VALERIE L. GIGLIO

Singing
IN MY
OWN
KEY
A VOCALIST'S TRIUMPH OVER STROKE

Singing In My Own Key: A Vocalist's Triumph Over Stroke
Copyright © 2016 by Valerie L. Giglio. All rights reserved.
First Print Edition: August 2016

For quantity ordering or special sales, please contact:

Forza Press
P.O. Box 3082
Wakefield, MA 01880
www.forzapress.com
info@forzapress.com

Published by Forza Press
Cover and Book Design by Streetlight Graphics, www.streetlightgraphics.com
Editing and writing consultation by Suzanne Sherman www.suzannesherman.com
Cover photo: © Kristin Gillis Photography www.kgillisphotgraphy.com
Back cover photo: © Vintage Girl Studios www.vintagegirlstudios.com

Library of Congress PCN: 2016903294
ISBN: 978-0-997-30780-1

I have tried to recreate events, locales and conversations from my memories of them. Some individual names have been changed to protect anonymity. Although every precaution has been taken to verify the accuracy of the information contained herein, the author and publisher assume no responsibility for any errors or omissions. No liability is assumed for damages that may result from the use of information contained within.

Printed in the United States of America
10 9 8 7 6 5 4 3 2 1

Introduction

LIFE IS ALL ABOUT CHOICES, including some with extremely uncertain outcomes. I faced such a choice at forty-two: Would I spend the rest of my life paralyzed, in a wheelchair and unable to even feed myself, or would I push my body and mind to the furthest limits of possibility and reclaim my life?

At forty-two years old, I suffered a devastating and life-threatening brain stem stroke that left me paralyzed on my left side, confined me to a wheelchair, caused my world to spin out of control, and stole my singing voice. Until the day of the stroke, I had lived a "normal" life. I had two working arms and legs. I ran up and down stairs. I did yard work. I wore high heels. I effortlessly did many seemingly inconsequential things and never gave them a second thought. And I did bigger things, too. I traveled the world. I had my own law practice. I enjoyed a successful career as a professional vocalist. I released two CDs and walked the red carpet at the Grammy Awards twice. I was a novice fencer and played the violin and the melodica. I had a dream life and a bright future.

Surviving that stroke, I learned that nothing is truly impossible. As I lay in a hospital bed unable to move a muscle and with a dangerous blood clot in my brain stem, I pined for the days I had walked normally, the days I had felt the breeze teasing my hair when I ran and the softness of the grass beneath my bare feet. I craved a return to the days I had enjoyed the silky glide of my fingers across the piano keys as I effortlessly sang the velvety tones of an Ella Fitzgerald song. It was an unrequited love of these simple things that impelled me and helped me ferociously claw my way from the depths of despair to the light again. Faith gave me the strength to weather the storm. My recovery is proof that miracles happen.

This is the story about a stroke that came out of nowhere and threatened a dream life and bright future. But more than that, it is the story of my triumph, achieving an almost complete recovery only one year later without even so much as a limp. I had reclaimed my life, and along the way, I learned to value every minute of it and to honor my soul's purpose.

Chapter One

I T WAS OPEN MIC NIGHT, November 2014. I stepped onto the stage at the Real School of Music wearing my black cut-out top and black vinyl pants, bright red lipstick, and my favorite piece of jewelry, an Italian choker in the shape of a cross. But anxiety pulsed through my body. Could I sing even one note?

I had sung on this stage only five months before, in June, and it wasn't a big deal to me then. I never had stage fright. That night, I was rehearsing a few retro soul songs for the Chick Singer Night Boston Showcase the following week, where I would be a featured performer. I was in the prime of my singing career and I stood on that stage like I owned it.

Tonight, everything was different.

I limped slightly as I walked across the stage, clinging to my friend Steven, my pianist for the evening, for support. My limp was more noticeable when I was nervous and I didn't want people to think there was anything wrong with me, so I tried to hide it.

A hush fell over the audience when Steven took a seat at the piano and started to play Charlie Chaplin's "Smile." I knew they anticipated the sound of my singing voice. I worried I would sound hoarse. Or weak. Or off-key. I had practiced every day for weeks, but I was a different person now. Anything could happen.

The last time I was on this stage, no one could have guessed that in a matter of a few hours the little girl with the big voice would suffer a massive stroke that would paralyze her entire left side and silence her singing voice. I had been to hell and back and here I was, about to sing, like I had done a thousand times before, like nothing had ever happened. I took a deep breath, looking into the faces of the people seated in the first couple of rows.

With my right hand, I grabbed the microphone from the stand and put it in my once completely paralyzed left hand, feeling a liberating sense of freedom. There was a chair nearby, but I planned to stand for as long as I could. I told the audience what happened to me since I was last here, how I had been on this stage one moment and later that same evening it seemed I had lost everything forever. The audience was in awe; a murmur of surprise rose from the seats.

And then I began to sing. Ahhh. I was home again. This was where my soul belonged. My treasured vocal coach, Vykki Vox, stood at the back of the room cheering me on as I sang the first verse. My voice was weak and I could only manage a few phrases before sitting down to catch my breath during the piano break. But I had done it. I sounded okay. The darkness of the last few months vanished and my spirit shone through the music of my voice, a voice I had thought was gone forever.

When Steven played the final chord, thunderous applause filled the performance room. I could see people clapping, cheering, standing up in their seats. Giddily, I spoke into the microphone, thanking everyone. Vykki ran to me, tears streaming from her eyes as she congratulated me. "I knew you could do it!"

And I had. I had done the impossible.

⁕

Sunday, June 1, 2014, was a gorgeous spring day in the suburbs of Boston, Massachusetts, and I was busy. I had a rehearsal to attend for a singing showcase where I was scheduled to perform in a few days. Later that same afternoon I would go to see my eight-year-old cousin Brooke perform in her dance recital.

A few days earlier, I lay in bed, trying to steal a few precious extra minutes of sleep before I had to get up and dress for a day in court with several clients. I slept on my right side, and I flopped over to my left very quickly at the sound of the alarm clock, turning my neck sharply.

As I jerked my body from right to left, still half-asleep, I felt a stinging and then unbearable pain in both sides of my neck. It literally took my breath away and I couldn't move for a few moments. I wanted to scream or cry out, but I didn't want to wake my husband, Mark, who was asleep next to me. It felt like a hundred knives were stabbing me in the neck all at once. I lay there, writhing in agony. I'd gotten a stiff neck many times from sleeping in the wrong position, yet there was something clearly different about this pain. It was worse than any I'd ever experienced. This will go away in a second, I kept repeating to myself, as the pain seared through my neck.

It didn't go away.

Over the next few days I went about my plan, working, shopping, preparing my garden and pool for the summer season, practicing my singing. I must have really pulled a muscle in my neck, I thought, as the pain continued, even worsened. Maybe I'd even sprained it or pinched a nerve. I decided to see a physical therapist to make sure I could move around the stage at the gig next weekend. Maybe I'd have to wear a neck collar for a week or so. I popped a pain reliever several times each day, though it didn't help much. The pain was back within a few hours.

I mentioned my neck ache to my parents when I visited them for dinner. I also complained about it to my husband. They thought it was no big deal. How could it be? People injure themselves much worse than this. I had probably slept the wrong way and I'd be fine in a day or two. Little did I know that by the following Monday, this little neck ache would change my life forever.

By Sunday, I was still in a fair amount of neck pain yet I attended my singing rehearsal. Dancing was difficult and I moved stiffly around the stage. My vocals sounded tired and weak, but I attributed this to the pain in my neck and continued singing my songs. After the rehearsal, I drove to pick up Mark and we left for Brooke's dance recital.

By the time I entered the school auditorium where the recital was taking place, the neck pain had intensified so much that I couldn't sit in my seat, and Mark stayed with me in the hallway.

The pain had become a constant burning sensation and was all I could focus on. I was clammy, exhausted, and listless.

"What if I have meningitis?" I asked Mark, nervous. "That causes a stiff neck." "You're okay," Mark replied. "You don't have a fever and you aren't sick. It's just a pulled muscle, but if you want, we can go the ER so you can get some peace of mind. The hospital is only a few blocks away."

We left the building without ever entering the auditorium.

Outside, I felt a blast of breezy, warm air. Summer was here, the sun was shining, and the weather was warm, but not too hot. I always loved the heat and the feeling of the sun beating down on me. But that day, the heat made me nauseous.

Mark would do anything for me, especially if he knew it would make me feel better emotionally. He didn't believe anything was wrong with me. I hadn't even had a cold for almost two years. He assumed we'd go to the hospital and I'd be assured that everything was fine.

We parked and entered the hospital, the same one I had used all of my life. I was born there. Every time I needed blood work or an X-ray, or when I had a bout of tonsillitis in my twenties, I went there. I trusted the medical staff. Unfortunately, before long I would know that going to that hospital that day would turn out to be the biggest mistake of my life.

Mark and I waited in the ER waiting area for what seemed like hours. I watched TV, barely able to turn to talk to Mark, who was sitting in the chair beside me. When I was finally called inside, the staff directed me to sit on a gurney in the ER hallway while I waited for a physician's assistant to examine me there. The rooms with beds were all occupied and it was a busy day in the ER.

A young woman in a white coat approached me and introduced herself as the afternoon physician's assistant. I could see she was in a hurry as she didn't do much of an exam on me; instead, she mostly just asked me a few simple questions. Did I have a fever? No. What had I been taking for the pain? Just over-the-counter pain relievers since Wednesday. Any other symptoms? "No," I said. "I'm just really tired and this pain won't go away."

I was one of *those* patients—a complainer, someone who

shouldn't waste the precious time of the ER staff with a little neck ache. She reassured me that I had a pulled muscle in my neck, probably from sleeping the wrong way, and gave me a prescription for painkillers. Then she sent me home.

I felt foolish. I had missed Brooke's recital because of a silly neck ache? My whole family was at the recital, even my elderly parents. And they all went to dinner afterward while I wasted all that time in the ER.

On the way home from the hospital, I stopped at a local supermarket for a tuna sandwich while Mark shopped for groceries and picked up some painkillers at the pharmacy next door. I walked the aisles feeling terribly tired and uneasy, but I chalked it up to the stress of the day and decided against taking the painkillers. I had a bad feeling about taking them.

That feeling, it would turn out, probably saved my life.

After a long, stressful day of singing, the dance recital, the hospital, and the supermarket, going home to relax was a much-needed relief. I didn't care that the house was a complete mess. I would clean it and cut off my ER bracelet in the morning, when I had more energy. I would call a physical therapist, too, to get rid of that kink in my neck. Mark gave me a kiss and went to play video games on the computer in our home office, which is directly across from our bedroom, and I curled up on the living room couch to watch a good disaster flick. In it there's a scene where one protagonist gets a life-threatening infection and another has to fight an impending Ice Age and wild animals in an apocalyptic New York City to get the necessary antibiotics. Things could be worse, I thought.

After the movie, I went to bed and drifted to sleep.

For the next few hours, I slept peacefully. Then, suddenly, I was jolted awake by violent dizziness. My room was spinning like Dorothy's house in *The Wizard of Oz*.

I was seeing double. I couldn't move my left hand, my left leg, my left foot, or my left arm. I could feel them, but I couldn't move them an inch. My entire left side was frozen. My right side felt as if it were floating. But at least I could move that side. My left arm was clenched in an awkward position, curled tightly to my chest, my fingers in a tight fist. My neck was in excruciating pain and my world was spinning.

What was happening to me?

I had been dizzy several times before, and I thought it was the worst feeling in the world. It scared the living hell out of me. Mostly, I got dizzy if I was overtired or hadn't been drinking enough water. These little spells only lasted a few seconds or minutes before going away. Now, the dizziness wasn't stopping.

I screamed for Mark, who was still on the computer just across the hall.

He hurried to my side. "What's wrong?" He bent closer to have a good look at me in the dark. Sometimes I talk in my sleep, so he thought I was still sleeping because I wasn't making much sense. Maybe I had a bad dream?

My left hand remained clenched in a fist and tightly frozen to my chest.

I opened my eyes wider and my focus jumped around the room: two television sets in my bedroom, two bureaus, two beds. "Get me my dizzy pills! Hurry!" I screamed.

Mark ran to the bathroom and grabbed the bottle of pills my doctor had prescribed for dizziness some years ago, which I kept on hand in case of an emergency. He put the pill bottle on my nightstand, but I couldn't reach for them. I was too dizzy. I couldn't see straight, and I had no left side.

About five minutes had elapsed and the room was still spinning out of control. I stared straight ahead at my bed and bureau, trying to focus the best I could. Everything was distorted; nothing seemed real.

Mark was still standing to the right of our bed, watching me with alarm. "Should I call 911?"

I nodded.

And that's when we both knew. Whatever was going on with me had to be pretty serious. Normally, I would never want to wake the neighborhood by calling an ambulance and making a scene. But this was different. I didn't know what was happening to me, and it wasn't good.

In minutes, I heard sirens outside my house. A police officer walked into our bedroom and took one look at the pill bottle Mark had placed on my nightstand. The officer had a look on his face. I knew that look from years of practice as a criminal lawyer. He probably assumed I had overdosed. I tried to tell him the pills were for anti-vertigo, but he had that "tough cop" stance, as if I should have been scared he would be arresting me for a drug-related offense. Here we were, a young couple with no children, living in a messy but otherwise very nice home. I was wearing a hospital bracelet. I could easily be mistaken for a drug addict and I know that was what this cop was likely thinking. Looking back, I would have thought the same thing.

I wanted to command the officer to get me to a hospital, but I was too dizzy and couldn't move my head or the left side of my body. The desire to tell him off took a back seat to my condition. The officer seemed annoyed. Maybe he thought I was having an anxiety attack or that I had some mental condition that made me think I was paralyzed. Maybe I was high on drugs.

Two paramedics arrived a few minutes later and I heard them wheel a stretcher inside our house. "What's going on?" they asked when they found me. One of them noticed I was wearing a hospital bracelet. "What happened that you had to go to the hospital?"

Fantastic, I thought. They're going to think I'm a drug addict, too.

"I can't move my left side, I'm very dizzy, and I can only see straight if I close one eye."

Mark told them he'd taken me to the ER a few hours earlier for neck pain and they sent me home with painkillers that I didn't take. The paramedics said they would take me back to the same ER. I told them again that I couldn't move, so the decision was made to take me via ambulance.

The next thing I knew, the paramedics loaded me onto a stretcher and wheeled me out of the bedroom. When they lifted the gurney to move me down the stairs, I almost threw up. I repeatedly recited my name and address in my head. I said it over and over again, reassurance that I still had my brain and that whatever was happening to me was only physical. I was terrified.

I'm going out in an ambulance. What is happening to me?

I just want to be okay. Please God, let me be okay. I began to panic.

I was paralyzed on my left side. I was seeing double. I was dizzy. All at the same time. These things only happen to people in horror movies or in *The Twilight Zone*, yet they were happening to me and for no apparent reason.

Remember when you were a kid and you listened to scary ghost stories on Halloween? Stories like, "There was this one guy, and he woke up with no arms or legs," or "All of a sudden, as the monster attacked, she opened her mouth to scream and nothing came out." Well, those creepy stories had become my reality. I was in a living hell and I couldn't run.

In the ambulance, the paramedics took my pulse and blood pressure. I was hooked up to an IV for fluids. I felt the stinging sensation of the IV enter my skin and the coolness of the fluid as it ran though my body. The paramedic thought I would feel better if I was hydrated.

I was still so scared. I begged the paramedic to stay with me in the ambulance. "I'm not going anywhere," he said, trying his best to calm me. My husband followed the ambulance in his car. He probably thought I would be coming home after a short trip to the ER and he wanted to have his car at the hospital. I wasn't so sure.

I wanted my husband. I wanted my mother. I wanted my father. Somebody.

I needed somebody to hold my hand and tell me that everything would be fine.

I started to feel afraid that I was going to die. I pleaded with God to let me be okay. I could only see the paramedic clearly if I closed one eye. Every bump in the road sent me into a vicious and merciless spin. When the vehicle turned a corner, it made my dizziness worse. I was also feeling excruciating neck pain, as if I was repeatedly being stabbed in both sides of my neck with an ice pick.

The paramedic radioed to dispatch. "I have a possible TIA here," I heard him say.

A TIA? Wasn't that a kind of stroke? Wasn't that something that happened to older people? All I knew was that one of my mom's friends had a TIA when she was in her seventies. I was forty-two.

Paralysis is a strange phenomenon. All of my limbs felt the same to me, except I couldn't move anything on my left side. My brain could not send the signal to move my entire left side at all, no matter how hard I tried. I willed my hand to move, but I got no response. Again, in my head I started to repeat my name and address. I knew what they were. I was still sane. I could think clearly. Phew! At least I had my brain.

After a ride that seemed to take hours, the ambulance arrived at the emergency room. By now, I was drifting in and out of consciousness, although I still knew what was going on around me. The hospital lights were incredibly bright and it was uncomfortable to see, even though I squinted one eye. Every few moments I opened my eyes and I saw so many people — a crowd of sorts, all dressed in white coats. Young doctors. Nurses. Everyone was scurrying around me yet it felt like I was waiting forever to get an answer about what was happening. Weakly, I managed to tell whoever would listen that I had been there just here a few hours ago and they had sent me home.

I could tell by their attitudes that they only half-believed my story. I may have been in rough shape, but I still had all my marbles. And I was getting sleepier by the second.

The experience of having a stroke is surreal. You're there, yet you aren't. Inside, you're screaming to get out, but you can't move. You can barely see. You can barely talk. A kind of emptiness envelops you, but at the same time, your brain is working on overdrive. It's been attacked and insulted and left wondering what the heck is going on.

The moments ticked by, and no one knew I was having a stroke. If I didn't get the treatment I needed to stop it from progressing, and soon, my survival was in jeopardy.

My brain cells were dying by the second, inching me closer and closer to a potential coma.

Eerily, I began to feel like I was floating in space, just slightly above my bed. I felt the bed sheets and the IV attached to my arm, but my mind was detached from my body, possibly entering a sort of self-preservation mode. I was able to move my right leg normally, but that too felt bizarre. It felt as light as a feather and at the same time weighed a ton. My mind was playing tricks on me and the connections in my brain were apparently going haywire. Nothing seemed real. Doctors shined lights into my eyes and asked me to follow a pencil they waved in front of my face.

I knew Mark was somewhere nearby, but the hospital wouldn't let him near me. The nausea and spinning were so extreme in addition to the paralysis of my left side, I felt I was in a carnival funhouse or tripping on some psychedelic drug. Nurses gave me an anti-nausea medication by IV, which kept me from vomiting, but that's not what I really needed. What I really needed was someone to stop a stroke, never mind stopping me from puking all over their clean floors. I couldn't move my left side. Not even a twitch. Even my head wouldn't turn. And that is how I lay on the bed in the ER, staring straight ahead for what seemed like an eternity.

Suddenly, I was rushed into another room and moved into a CT scan machine. I was not fully conscious but I saw those lights hanging above me in the room, lights so bright it was agonizing to look at them or even keep one eye open, so I shut both eyes. A nurse held my hand as the loud humming and buzzing of the CT machine began.

I had no fear of what was happening to me. Everything around me turned a bright white and became dark at the same time. The voices of the doctors and nurses sounded like they were in a vacuum. Distorted. The noise was terribly loud, but I wasn't fazed. I just wanted to sleep. I drifted in and out of consciousness.

Had I have been given a CT scan with injectable dye, it would have shown the tears in my vertebral arteries. But I wasn't given a scan using injectable dye, and as a result, the CT scan showed everything was normal. On paper, there was nothing wrong with me.

Mark appeared beside me along with an ER nurse when I was being wheeled back to the ER examination room. "Don't worry," she said. "You aren't having a stroke. It's probably an allergic reaction, or a seizure." Her tone was calm, even reassuring.

I didn't believe her. Did they honestly believe I was having a seizure that lasted hours on end? How was that even possible? How could I have had an allergic reaction to tuna and Popsicles, which I ate all the time? I had a sudden burst of energy and became more alert.

I had one chance, and this was it. I didn't want to die, not now anyway, and certainly not at the hands of these clowns. So much time had been wasted by this hospital and I wasn't about to let them finish up by killing me.

It took all of my energy to raise my voice beyond a whisper, but I mustered up all my strength to lethargically murmur to the ER nurse that I didn't ingest anything other than a tuna sandwich and a Popsicle earlier that evening. I wasn't allergic to tuna or Popsicles. And I didn't have a history of seizures. There was no response besides a nod of her head.

Mark stood by my bedside as I continued to be held in limbo at the hospital, each second sending me along a path to further destruction of brain cells. The medical staff was apparently finished trying to figure things out, so they allowed Mark to be with me in the exam room.

Mark didn't want to call and wake my parents, who are nearing eighty and would have been exceedingly worried about their only daughter being oddly unable to move or see straight, especially after they had just seen me a few hours earlier. Mark said he'd call them in the morning, once this was over with, we were home again, and after we had slept in. He was frightened for me, but he did an excellent job at pretending to be tough about the whole situation.

Despite the normal test results, by now I had developed a significant facial droop on my left side. Nothing about me was symmetrical. My left lip pointed downward. My tongue slanted to the right. This should have raised an alarm that a stroke or a stroke-related event was occurring.

Doctors and interns shuffled in and out at their leisure, although all I could see were glimpses of white coats or flashlights waved in front of my eyes. One youthful man in a white coat told me to make a fist or grab his hand with my left one, and I couldn't. I tried to follow the path of his fingers across the room, but I couldn't do that either.

Suddenly, a nurse pulled back the curtain in my exam room. "You're being transferred to Massachusetts General Hospital because we don't have an MRI machine here," she said matter-of-factly.

No MRI machine? She must have been joking. What kind of hospital has no MRI machine? Of course they had an MRI there. Apparently they didn't use it after regular business hours.

I wanted to get out of that horrid place as soon as I could. I couldn't sit idly by while my life lay in the balance and every second my symptoms seemed to be worsening. I needed something, an explanation, medication—something! C'mon! Was this situation so difficult to figure out? My symptoms were obvious even to me and I was only half-awake. Surely, one of these physicians had to know what was going on!

After what seemed like forever, I was finished wasting any more precious time with this suburban sideshow masquerading as a hospital. I was wheeled out on a stretcher into the cool air of an early summer night, and loaded into the back of an ambulance.

No one seemed in a rush. Paramedics drove me to MGH at the usual speed without the siren. Who was I to them? Some girl having a bad anxiety attack? A mental delusion?

Mark rode in the passenger seat of the ambulance, making idle chatter with the driver. I heard them from the rear of the ambulance and thought, if they're talking this casually, I must be fine.

The ambulance arrived at Mass General and I was whisked into the ER, where doctors, nurses and ambulance staff surrounded me. But I was being treated differently here, that was obvious. These people clearly knew there was something seriously wrong, and I was a priority.

I was rushed into the room with the MRI machine. The lights were so bright and the MRI's excruciatingly loud clanking sound pierced my brain. I had a blank feeling as I started losing consciousness again. I shut my eyes and tried to imagine I was drifting off to a serene, worry-free place, but I could only visualize a blank page in my mind. My brain couldn't imagine anymore.

The brain is a strange and complex organ. I had read about people who suffer various unspeakable nightmares in horrific accidents yet strangely remain calm in the face of it all. I always wondered how that was even possible. How could a person remain calm if their arm was bitten off by a shark? Or their leg was severed from their body in a car accident? The brain has remarkable coping mechanisms. And so, while I lay on that gurney in the MRI, the best I can say is I went into a strange relaxation mode. I would call it an almost near-death experience. My brain was trying to cope the only way it knew how to. In this most nerve-wracking and anxious time of my life, all I wanted to do was sleep.

My next memory is of being wheeled quickly into the neurology ICU. As I was sped through the hallway of the unit, I remember being impressed with the newness and the high-tech atmosphere. I didn't seem to have a care about much else. In any other circumstance my ferociously type A personality would have been in overdrive. Now, I was like a drugged-out hippie in the land of Weirdsville, languishing in some strange semiconscious state of awareness.

And there was Mark again! He appeared suddenly beside my bed as I arrived in an ICU room. I had no idea how he got there, or how I got there, for that matter. I only remembered bits and pieces of the ambulance ride, the MRI, and being wheeled to the ICU.

Mark told me he called my parents and they were at the hospital and had spoken to the doctor handling my case, Dr. Aneesh Singhal.

Dr. Singhal was a neurologist from the Massachusetts General Hospital Stroke Service and a basically all-around amazing man. He wore a suit instead of a lab coat, he spoke with a slight Indian accent, and his manner was gentle. I trusted him from the outset.

Dr. Singhal explained what had happened to me hours earlier. I'd torn the arteries in my neck at some point in the last few days and the bleeding caused a blood clot to form, leading to a stroke in my brain stem.

A stroke.

Chapter Two

THE WEEKS LEADING UP TO my stroke were like a prelude to a nightmare. After a long and arduous Boston winter, I'd been excited by the thought of leaving the house without a coat or winter boots. The days were longer, and I was giddy with excitement as winter turned to spring. I had big plans for the summer: I would be going to Berklee College of Music in Umbria, Italy, in July.

That was the year I decided I wanted to incorporate a musical instrument into my singing. I had played violin for years, but I wanted to learn another instrument, one I could use while performing on stage, in the musical breaks in my songs. In May, Mark gave me a melodica, a small handheld keyboard with a mouthpiece. The instrument sounds something like a saxophone yet is played something like a piano. It was perfect. I played it for hours on end.

I was ecstatic. In two months I'd be roaming around Italy with my melodica and singing on street corners during the Umbria Jazz Festival. I'd be immersed in Berklee's renowned educational program. At night, I would jam with some of the other students at one of the jazz clubs in Perugia. Right away, I learned Cannonball Adderley songs and I played Procol Harum's "Whiter Shade of Pale."

I also planned to be a part of Chick Singer Night, a musician's showcase with many chapters around the United States. Chick Singer Night features concert performances for female musicians, and I had participated in one of these concerts a few years earlier. I was thrilled to be on their Boston program again. It was the tenth

15

anniversary show, and I devoted hours to mapping out the details of my performance. Maybe I could even use the melodica.

I'd recently started to record some original material for a CD, but my songs weren't ready to be performed in public yet. Instead, I would do a 1960s retro soul set with an Amy Winehouse vibe. I would sing an Otis Redding cover and songs by The Shirelles and Etta James. I found a sexy, retro leopard-accented stretch dress with elbow-length gloves, my signature style on stage. I was never one for a conservative look.

Before long, I was all over social media in an advertisement for the show, along with several other featured women performers. My family and friends bought advance tickets. It was going to be an incredible night of music.

The rehearsal took place a few days before the show, giving me some time to work with the house band I'd be performing with. Rehearsal had been difficult as my neck was throbbing and sore, and I was feeling lethargic. Days of severe neck pain took a toll on my energy and on my singing voice. I couldn't belt out the songs, or even sing very loudly. I barely got through the songs. I couldn't move much on stage, either. If I had to turn around to talk to the band, I did it like a robot. And I sounded hoarse. When I bent to pick up my water bottle, the pain was excruciating. Every move I made hurt. I sang like a statue, afraid to move, which was out of character for me. I'm always dancing around on stage.

"Don't worry, guys," I assured the band and my friends Jennifer and Marcia, who were also the show's directors. "I'll go to physical therapy this week. It's probably just a pulled muscle or neck strain. I'll be fine by the show."

I never made it to the show. I spent the evening of Chick Singer Night in a bed at Mass General.

A life without music is simply unfathomable to me. Singing and music are part of my soul, they are part of who I am. All of my experiences, good and bad, are set to my own soundtrack. Love, pain, fear — all of these emotions are alive in my soul and giving them an outlet for expression makes me feel truly alive. A life without music would be a life without dimensional depth.

My earliest memories involve music—singing and dancing in my living room as a young child, pretending a hairbrush was a microphone. I always wanted to be famous, to make records and perform on stage in front of thousands of people. Even as a little girl, the thought of being on stage was exhilarating. When I was four years old, my mother enrolled me in ballet classes at Miss Ashenden's School of Dance in Wakefield, Massachusetts. The teacher, who must have been ninety years old, had a very tough demeanor. It seemed she would put me in a torture chamber if I didn't point my toes. A long, lanky woman with zero interpersonal skills, I think at one point she even told my mother I was ding-toed. But I didn't care. I carried my little box of ballet shoes as I ran up a high and imposing staircase to my lesson every week. The goal? The performance.

Every year, I waited all year with bated breath for this event with all the stage makeup, costumes and bright lights. I loved it all, even the industrial smell of the 1970s-style junior high school auditorium where the dance school held recitals. That smell could only mean one thing: I'd soon be a star in front of my adoring fans, which consisted of my parents, grandparents, and the other children's families. Every year I'd get so excited I couldn't contain myself.

From the first time our class took the stage I knew that performing was what I was meant to do. I belonged in front of an audience. No matter how nervous I was, the moment I stepped onstage and the music began to play, I became a star in my own world.

My childhood best friend, Carolann, lived across the street. She was my creative collaborator, as we spent most of our afternoons planning our variety shows and plotting our next stage production. We sang, danced, and even acted. Once we wrote a short play about a count and some stolen jewels and we sold tickets to our families to come and see it. I had a swimming pool at my house and we spent hours having underwater tea parties and mapping out the theme for our next show. We had to keep things lively so our parents would stay interested.

I first learned about music from my elementary school music teacher, Mr. Rizza.

Our class met in the school gym for weekly music class and Mr. Rizza passed out mimeographed music sheets of various songs for us to learn to sing. A mimeograph machine was the precursor to the copy machine, still in use in the early 1980s. A student was usually assigned to go to the front office to "run off" copies one by one for the entire class. Running off copies involved turning a crank on a machine the size of a small car. The sheets would be hot, damp, and smell awesome.

Singing came naturally to me. The first song I sang was "Dear Hearts and Gentle People," while Mr. Rizza explained the concept of notes and rests to us. "A man that tips his hat upside down is only a half-gentleman," he'd say, referring to a half rest on a music staff. Most of the class just yelled the lyrics, and a good number of my classmates seemed to be tone deaf. Many of them went on to become athletes in high school while several of us became musicians.

I looked forward to music class every week and couldn't wait to see what we'd do next. In third grade, one day Mr. Rizza told us we could all learn to play an instrument the following year if we wanted to sign up for classes. How exciting that was—my chance to really learn about music. I had always been instantly thunderstruck by every musical instrument I saw, and now I got to choose one to learn to play! I chose the violin because it seemed like a great way to learn to read sheet music. I joined the school orchestra and later the choir.

At first we barely screeched out a rendition of "Ode to Joy," but by high school we were playing complex arrangements of the great classical masterpieces. I sang in the chorus and show choir.

Although I had big musical ambitions, I was also quite studious. I knew the job prospects for musicians were highly competitive and I needed to do something that would bring in a lot of money. I'd had an entrepreneurial spirit all my life—in fact, I remember my cousin Tommy and I selling string beans from my grandfather's garden to his neighbors, and once we turned my parents' basement into a haunted house and charged our family admission. My parents paid an admission fee to our haunted house just to get to their own basement.

The defining moment when I decided to become a lawyer happened when I was seventeen years old and a junior in high school. The year was 1989 and I was working part-time in the jewelry department of the now-defunct Service Merchandise. My co-workers were mostly a mixture of teenagers like me, as well as some older folks looking to earn some extra cash. On the first day of the job I noticed that all the ladies who worked in my department fawned over an impeccably dressed young man and fellow jewelry sales associate named Paul. Curious about why they were huddled in the storeroom of the department like a football team secretly discussing their next play, I listened in on their chatter.

"What a catch that Paul will be," one lady said.

"He's going to be a lawyer," another lady said. "Whoever gets to be with him will be a very lucky girl."

Hmmm, I thought. Who was this Paul person? And what did he have that I didn't?

I certainly didn't need to land a "catch." No, thank you. I was determined to be just as much of a "catch" as Paul, to have all the boys wishing they could be with *me*, not the other way around. It irked me that just because I was a young girl no one thought of me in the same way they would a guy. I could be a lawyer, too! I'd be darned if anyone was going to tell me I had to land a successful man to achieve success. *I* would be the catch.

I always looked for the most challenging paths. I was like a sponge for knowledge and law seemed the perfect challenge for me. I dreamed of captivating an entire courtroom with my presence. I would accept nothing less. Other jobs seemed boring to me.

After graduating from high school, I studied accounting at Salem State University because I wanted a major that would get me accepted into law school, and I wasn't keen on political science. Accounting was more in line with my entrepreneurial bent. With an accounting background, I could possibly become a tax lawyer and earn enough to fund my musical endeavors. If I were a lawyer, there would be no limit to what I could do. I could be a famous singer, and I could read or draft my own recording contracts. I might even start my own record label. While my friends enjoyed days at the beach and went to fun parties, I spent months tirelessly studying for the LSAT entrance exam for law school.

Ultimately I went to New England Law School by day, and at night and on weekends I practiced and taught vocal lessons from my parents' basement. I was the lead singer of a local dance band, and we played in a friend's garage or at the occasional pub on weekends. My life was filled with dreams and ideas and I was brimming with excitement thinking of the possibilities that lay ahead.

During my final year of law school, because of my degree in accounting, I was able to get an interview with a major accounting firm. For a few short weeks leading up to that interview I began to think I could be destined for a desk job as a tax lawyer, and the musical career I wanted so badly was never going to happen. With this in mind, on the day of the interview I dressed in a conservative suit and eyeglasses, with my briefcase in hand. Sitting in the reception area as I waited to be called in, I started having mixed feelings. I knew I was one of only a half-dozen or so job-seeking student candidates for a swanky tax attorney position that probably paid a ridiculously high salary. While I was genuinely grateful for the opportunity to be selected as a candidate for this position, in my heart I knew it was a mistake and that the job wasn't for me.

My thoughts were interrupted when I heard my name called. As I entered the office, I was greeted by a short rotund man with glasses. He must have been five years older than me but he looked like he was pushing sixty. He spoke in a monotone, and at one point he asked if I had any hobbies. I told him I was a singer and I taught a few students at night or on Saturday mornings. He frowned. "I'm concerned," he said, "about your singing. I'm afraid it will interfere if you were given a job with our firm." I explained that

I only taught a few students and that it was not going to stop me from working full-time. "This is the sort of thing that's frowned upon in our firm. It could distract you from the job." That's all it took. No one tells me what to do, and certainly I wasn't about to allow a stranger to demand I give up singing. Singing was my life! Law was a backup plan that I believed would work in conjunction with my music, not destroy my dreams. Then and there, I decided I would work for myself and open my own law practice. I walked out of that interview a few minutes later, somewhat relieved. Yes, I wasn't going to get the job, but I was actually happy about that. I was not going to become anyone's slave, no matter how much they paid me. It might not be an easy road, but I would make my own rules. No one would ever dictate my professional behavior or my career path. Life is too short not to follow your dreams and I was determined to achieve all of them.

The path to becoming a lawyer required that I sacrifice many years of my young adult life to school and to studying. With years of never-ending homework and lugging twenty pounds of books on the subway every day, it seemed like I was always in school. Many times I thought this grind, this torture, would be my life forever, but I knew I had to keep going and never look back if I wanted to be a success. That same determination, ambition and drive, with school and with music, would one day get me out of a wheelchair and walking again.

Chapter Three

I WILL NEVER FORGET DR. SINGHAL and his amazing attitude. As I lay almost motionless in the ICU at Mass General, Dr. Singhal gave me the first glimmer of hope that I might someday return to the "old me." If *he* wasn't freaking out, I figured I had a chance.

The other doctors seemed nervous and tentative. Some of them treated me like a stroke patient on a "need-to-know" basis while scurrying in and out of my room in the ICU, always cautious not to give me false hope of recovering. Every time I dared to ask whether I was going to be normal again, the response from the other doctors was always the same: "We hope for the best," or "No one can predict these things."

Dr. Singhal seemed to be the only doctor who didn't use the "cover your ass" route in communicating with me. He anticipated a full recovery in twelve to eighteen months. More important, he was the first to give me any indication that recovery was even possible. It was exactly what I needed, and I desperately clung to the belief that things were going to get better.

Most people believe a stroke only happens to the elderly or people with heart problems, but that's not the case. In rare instances, a stroke can result from the tearing of arteries in the neck that supply blood and oxygen to the brain—a vertebral artery dissection—which is what happened to me. *Both* of my arteries dissected, one on each side of my neck. In my case, however, my vertebral arteries were not torn because of any type of trauma. There had been no car accident, no severe neck movements or jolts. No one will ever know for certain the reason why. I was in excellent health. I simply turned my neck to look at my alarm clock and the severe neck pain that often accompanies an arterial tear began. The arteries tore and began to bleed internally. Over the course of several days my body worked feverishly to stop the bleeding by clotting my blood. Once a clot formed, it traveled to my brain stem and gave me a stroke. The brain stem controls all of the major functions of the body including regulating blood pressure, breathing, heart rate, and motor control. A stroke in this part of the brain can be life-ending.

All of this information was so utterly terrifying and outrageous that I couldn't quite wrap my head around it. It seemed like a far-fetched, made-up disorder you would find on some wacko medical show on cable TV at three a.m. or when you were surfing the Net and stumbling on websites for hypochondriacs.

In despair I asked God and the Universe how the act of turning my neck could give me a stroke. What kind of joke was this? I had twisted my neck numerous times in my life, I mean, *really* twisted. I had danced for years, craning my neck in ballet or jazz dance routines, and I was fine. I had even break-danced in the 1980s, contorting my neck in an effort to copy moves I saw in *Flashdance*. Nothing bad happened. In high school I was a Pom-Pom girl and I moved my neck sharply all the time doing cheerleader-style routines. At the local gym, I lifted weights for twenty years without any problems. I swam in my pool and did all sorts of yard work. At the hair salon, I'd happily dropped my head backwards into the shampoo bowl hundreds of times. Yet something as trivial as turning my head to see the clock tore my neck arteries and led to a stroke. How was it even possible?

This entire state of affairs was so incomprehensible, like having a heart attack from dropping a fork on the floor, or going blind from turning the bathroom light on in the dark. I felt like I was in that old *Twilight Zone* episode where the townspeople can't think bad thoughts about the neighborhood kid or he'd wish them into a cornfield. I was definitely in the cornfield, that's for sure. The cornfield of the truly bizarre.

What was I going to do now? I had no plan. I had that small flicker of hope from Dr. Singhal and that was it.

I was a very spiritual and religious person, and after the stroke I became afraid of it all. I avoided anything remotely spiritual in nature. I knew that a lot of friends and family were praying for me and I felt terrible because it seemed like I didn't appreciate it, even though I really did. I just couldn't express it. I was too scared. What if my spirituality had caused my stroke? What had I done to make God angry with me? It had to be something pretty bad. What if I wasn't religious enough? As ridiculous as that sounded, I was beginning to believe I'd brought this stroke on myself. I had no other answers as to what really caused my neck arteries to dissect on both sides. Maybe it was the result of some spiritual forces, I thought, lying in the hospital, paralyzed on my left side.

Until that point, my religion and spirituality were important aspects of my identity. Then they vanished overnight. Prior to the stroke, I went to church every Sunday and God was an important part of my life. I had asked God for help so many times in my life. What if I'd asked for too much help in the past and God became offended? Maybe I shouldn't have asked Him to help me to successfully graduate from law school? Or guide me in my music career? I had morphed into someone terror-stricken by anything spiritual. I simply shut off that part of myself. I didn't pray. I wiped out every religious or spiritual part of me that existed. How could God allow this to happen to me in the first place? Maybe I was being punished for liking some spiritual concepts and going to metaphysical bookstores in my spare time. I felt empty inside. I didn't want to hear about anything related to New Age. I was afraid of it. What if I thought of some wise, spiritual quote and it gave me another stroke?

What I didn't realize was that the will to live originated in my faith. And that will emanated from my love of spirituality and God. I was blessed with many gifts. I was the singer, the dancer, the lawyer, the violinist, and the spiritual person who loved life and loved to travel. I was complex. I loved everyone in my life and I did as many things as I could squeeze into a day. I enjoyed many adventures. I loved all the holidays and being with my family. I loved going to church on Sundays. I cherished all of my friendships. I had a big personality and a near-constant smile. Yet, in one day, I became none of those things. I was a shell. A hollow person. It was like someone had come and emptied out my personality overnight.

It's amazing how life can change so quickly. Almost everything I acquired over forty-two years by simply being me had disappeared in a flash. I got a taste of what life had to offer and it was all taken away in the blink of an eye. My life was stolen from me like a thief in the night, creeping away with so much of what had made me who I was. It was as if someone had come along with a giant eraser and wiped out my entire existence but left me still alive to witness the aftermath. My personality, my walk, my talk, my singing talent, my vision, my hand — all of it was taken away from me, right from under my nose one June night. It was as if someone had mercilessly torn my vibrant, healthy, successful life away from me at the age of forty-two and replaced it with a life of severe disability, despair, and around-the-clock nursing care. Every dream I had for my future seemed like I'd had it a lifetime ago. There would be no more singing, no more dancing. No more lawyering. No more evening strolls around the neighborhood or Lake Quannapowitt in Wakefield with my husband, holding his hand. No more shopping with my mother. No more going to church on Sunday mornings or visits with my family and friends. No more happiness. I was devastated, thinking that the rest of my life would be spent in a wheelchair or a walker, leaving the house only for doctors' appointments and to go to therapy. It wasn't fair.

What on earth was I going to do now?

Thoughts like these continued to race through my brain. In my mind I saw images of my childhood, and I pined for those days. Those were carefree days when I had the use of both hands. I recalled playing Barbies with Carolann after elementary school, dressing our dolls in the latest styles. I remembered riding our bikes through the neighborhood and putting on those music and dance shows for our families. I remembered going to violin lessons on Morrison Road in Wakefield over the summer break when I was in junior high and high school. I had both hands then, too. I drove my 1978 Pontiac Bonneville to Revere Beach with my friends in the late 1980s. I danced in recitals every year. I spent many afternoons visiting my grandmother and running up and down the stairs at her house.

I couldn't even cry about those memories. And I had always been a very emotional and sensitive person. I guessed the stroke had taken that away, too.

But there was one thing the stroke hadn't taken away: my will. My will was possibly the strongest trait I had. Drive and motivation were the forces behind almost everything I had done since I was born. And they were still there, in the back of my mind, ready to be unleashed at the time I needed them the most.

I was an only child, born to Italian-American parents, and raised in Wakefield, Massachusetts, a few miles north of Boston. My father, a Navy vet — turned avionics man — turned educator, always encouraged me to be ambitious and to set and achieve my goals. To this day he stands behind me in everything I do and regularly reminds me of what I am capable of doing if I put my mind to it.

Besides having my father's constant encouragement and support, I inherited a tough attitude from my mother. My mother doesn't take guff from anyone, and though she is kind and sweet and stands no more than five feet tall in heels, she's feisty. If anyone had the perfect family background for conquering the effects of a debilitating stroke and kicking it in the pants until victory was won, it was me.

I learned a lot about myself while lying in the ICU. I learned that if my will was still there, I *could* get my life back. It would be a long road, but maybe, just maybe, I could do it. I wanted to really live again and not simply exist, floating in a sea of empty, blank space. I didn't want to fall down a rabbit hole.

Maybe there was a reason I'd always had so much ambition and drive. Maybe it was to prepare me for this, the greatest battle I would ever endure. I began to daydream. I imagined myself wearing shorts, my hair in a ponytail, just bopping along through the hospital halls in the white wedge sneakers I bought in Italy, jangling my car keys in my hand after driving myself to a follow-up appointment.

"Beep…beep…beep… beep…"

Those sounds jarred me back to reality, with all the machines I was connected to from my hospital bed. But something monumental had just happened. That daydream I'd just had told me everything I needed to know. I could do it. There would be no more "woe is me." I had to focus on rebuilding myself. And with that, I began the first page of rewriting my life.

Chapter Four

FTER GRADUATING FROM LAW SCHOOL and passing the bar exam in the late 1990s, I opened my own law practice and started taking cases. I won my first jury trial on my first criminal case. In the months leading up to my trial I appeared in court for various issues related to the case. I was green and inexperienced, but I acted like I owned the courtroom.

The district attorney's office at that time consisted of mostly young people. One assistant district attorney in particular graduated from my law school and would later get axed from the department for unethical shenanigans. He often pretended to be friendly to me when all along I knew he'd been talking about me behind my back and telling the other assistant district attorneys that they'd win any jury trial against me with their hands tied behind their backs. He thought I was a bit of an airhead. Maybe it was the way I dressed, or that I looked like I was twelve and had hardly any legal experience. But when I heard that, I knew I could win the case in a heartbeat. I knew exactly what I was doing. And if the prosecutor thought I was a bit of an airhead it could work to my advantage. It was part of the master plan. It was sheer genius. And it worked.

My client was a young guy who'd been beaten up by a rogue dirty cop at a local strip joint but he was being charged with assaulting an officer. The trial hinged on the testimony of key witnesses, including the defendant's aunt, who kept referring to the club as "The Jiggly Room." I pulled out all the stops on this trial. Enlisting the guidance of a seasoned colleague, I crafted an opening statement and closing argument that Perry Mason would bow down to. The client had a history of criminal charges and run-ins with the police, so the government was looking for a lot of jail time. I won the trial after the jury deliberated for only an hour. I saved the client from certain jail time and won him his freedom. Afterwards, he asked me on a date. I had put my arm on his back during the trial, to evoke sympathy from the jury and humanize the guy. He probably thought this meant I wanted to sleep with him! I let him know I was not interested, and I was sufficiently grossed out for the next ten years.

And then there was the *pièce de résistance*: I was assigned to a criminal case for a client who was doing hard time for sexual offenses. I represented him on some paperwork issues after he was already incarcerated. Apparently, he fell in love with me, repeatedly calling my office to tell me how pretty I looked in court. Not good.

After it become clear that he was no longer calling for legal advice on his case, I tried to ignore the calls, or at least pretend I was too busy to talk. Several months later I opened my mail to read a Christmas card from him, along with a poem declaring his love for me. It was called "A Thugg in Love." ("Thugg" was spelled with an extra "g" just for added dramatic effect, I suppose.) He told me we were meant to be together, how thoughts of me got him through his days behind bars, that I was a lion in court with the heart of a lamb. Sensitive, for a convicted rapist! He wrote about how he would find me as soon as he was released from prison. Great, I thought. A rapist is in love with me and vows to find me when he's out of prison. Just what I need. Aggravated, I called the jail and a tough female correctional officer promised she'd send him a message to cut the nonsense with me. Needless to say, he never bothered me again.

Even though I was busy with an ever-growing caseload, I never stopped singing. I joined a classic rock band as the lead singer for a few years before meeting the man who would change my musical life forever.

The man's name was Al Vega. Al was a Boston jazz legend and a friend and colleague to people I met only in my dreams, people like Count Basie, Nina Simone, Dinah Washington, and

Liberace, to name just a few. My friend Kathy, another musician, had told me about this local legend named Al Vega who taught piano out of his home in Everett, not too far away. At that time I was looking for piano lessons because I wanted to accompany myself on future gigs.

I found Al Vega's number in the telephone book and called him. I explained my situation, what I was looking for. Al treated me like an old friend immediately and invited me to come and sing a song at his next gig — that weekend. I went to the gig, which was at an Italian restaurant in East Boston. Al was playing with his jazz trio. I was a little nervous as I had never sung with a professional jazz trio before. I was used to singing with rock bands, and an electric guitar can mask mistakes. In a jazz trio, vocals are distinct, front and center. In this band, there would be piano, upright bass, and drums. I chose to sing Etta James' song, "At Last." I had performed the song at home and at karaoke bars many times, and I knew the melody well. That song would go on to become one of my signature songs.

Al's piano playing was the best I'd ever heard. He was a virtuoso, often playing a barrage of notes at a million miles an hour. That night, after I sang "At Last," Al asked me for some more songs. I didn't have anything else prepared, but I was able to wrangle my way through "My Funny Valentine" and a few more tunes he played. I discovered the world of performing jazz standards and I loved it.

Before long, I became one of Al's jazz vocalists and he took me under his wing, teaching me about the stylistic and business sides of jazz singing and introducing me to many great artists on the Boston music scene.

Al taught me a lot of important life lessons. He taught me that sometimes we have to take a chance and keep going no matter what obstacles we face. Nothing stopped Al.

He performed almost nightly until his death at ninety years old. He never let anything prevent him from playing his music. He knew that, for him, stopping the music would be a death sentence worse than any illness.

In some way, I believe I was destined to meet Al. When I visited him in the hospital after he suffered a heart attack in his eighties, he was making arrangements to bring in his trio and play a jazz gig for the other patients. He booked gigs from his bed. I vowed that if I faced medical problems in my later years, I would be just like him. Al taught me how valuable music is to the human spirit. By example, he showed me what it was like to never give up. I never could have guessed it would be only twelve years later when I'd need that attitude to challenge a war raging inside my body.

It was all making sense. My life was clearly on a preordained path. Everything I had done, all of my influences, from my mother and father to Al Vega, my drive and all of my accomplishments — everything was preparing me to overcome the effects of this horrific stroke and reclaim my life. I needed those experiences to illuminate my path.

Until that time, I believed my goal in life was to be a successful singer and lawyer. It wasn't. All the paths in my life were leading me to this one road: to conquer my disabilities.

The days in the hospital passed as an endless continuum of staring straight ahead into space. Nurses constantly shuffled in and out. My parents, Mark, Mark's mother, or other close family members visited daily. It was hard to look at them unless I wore an eye patch to stop the double vision. And I still had the constant stabbing neck pain from the torn arteries.

A PICC line was attached to my arm. (PICC stands for "peripherally inserted central catheter," and a PICC line is like a beer tap for IVs, so to speak.) I looked like something out of an episode of the TV medical show *House*, hooked up to machines and receiving fluids, blood thinners, pain medications and tranquilizers all day long.

I never even attempted to swallow in those early days. I don't think it even crossed my mind. The drugs I was given often made me feel loopy enough that I didn't care about swallowing, so I never gave it any thought. I had too many other things to worry about. I only realized I couldn't swallow when a hospital speech therapist visited me. She made me drink a glass of water in front of her and the water spilled all over my chin. Then I got ferociously dizzy.

"I'm so dizzy! Please help me!" I yelled.

The effort it took for me to put that cup to my mouth was equivalent to spending hours at the gym. I was quickly sedated with an injection of anti-anxiety medication to calm me and, hopefully, stop the spinning. I felt like I had run a marathon and passed out.

Dr. Singhal visited me every morning to see how I was doing. In my first few days in the ICU, he told me and my parents that I might need an angiogram, where they'd insert a catheter in my groin and get into my neck arteries that way. Dr. Singhal decided to hold off on this procedure in case the blood thinners began to work. I was too shocked by the idea of this to even comprehend it was happening to me.

A procedure in my neck arteries? Near my brain? Would I be able to think again?

Would I lose my intelligence? Would I even know who I was when I came out of it? I had all sorts of scary thoughts. I had just begun to breathe life back into the blank slate I had become. I didn't want this to be like a medieval lobotomy and leave me drooling into a bib forever.

I knew that strokes often killed older people or left them permanently disabled and with a twisted face and mumbled speech, confined to a wheelchair or to using a walker and staying indoors or in a nursing home for the rest of their lives, which typically wasn't too long. I refused to suffer that fate.

My only personal experience with strokes involved my grandmother, who had a stroke in her late seventies, when I was a teenager. After it, she walked with a three-pronged cane for the rest of her life and she slowed considerably from the spry person I had always known her to be. She couldn't drive, she walked at a snail's pace, wore orthopedic-looking sneakers, and she often required a wheelchair in public. But she was as smart as a whip. And she had fun. She didn't let her infirmity stop her.

I missed my grandmother. I wished she was with me. Her

spirit always was, but I wanted her company, in person, at my bedside. And I missed Al Vega. What I wouldn't have given to see him again. I thought of what they'd both done in their later years and how they survived and thrived. I wanted to share their attitude toward life.

Every thought of someone making their way through a shit-storm and coming out like a flower on the other side was breathing the life back into me a little bit at a time, though my fears were still very intense. I needed a lot courage to face the fear of dying, the fear of never being able to walk or sing again, the fear I'd never be able to work again, my newfound fear of anything spiritual, and my fear of the unknown. And those were just the top fears. I had so many.

Fear is strange. It festers and grows. It can get out of control and take over your life. Fear can eat away at you and strip you of confidence. It can destroy everything you've worked for and hold you back in ways you can't even begin to imagine.

I knew the key to removing my fears and reaching my potential without anything getting in the way is to run and never look back. About ten years ago, when we were at a Red Sox game at Fenway Park, my father told me, "Always look ahead. Never look back. What happens if you look back? You stumble. But if you keep moving ahead, you can see where you're going." I never forgot that. I had to look ahead without anything holding onto the back of my shirt.

Chapter Five

IN 2009 I RECORDED MY first CD, "Songbook." It was a collection of jazz standards, with the Al Vega Trio backing me. My main reason for recording this CD was that Al was approaching ninety and I knew he wouldn't live forever. I wanted to record with him while he was still making music.

I chose to record songs with a special meaning to me. I wanted songs that spoke to my soul. "I Left My Heart in San Francisco" was a dedication to my grandmother's brother Joe and was the first track on the CD. Uncle Joe played alto saxophone and that was his signature song. I recorded "Autumn Leaves" for my grandmother. For years, she had told me how she wanted that song to be sung at her funeral. I thought of her every time I performed it with Al. When she passed away in 2006, I was heartbroken. I spent a long time thinking of all the things I could have done differently while she was still alive to show her how much I loved her.

Two years later, I followed "Songbook" with a CD of songs in Italian called "The Italian Project." I had always been obsessed with Italy, my Italian heritage, the language, and the culture. For years, I had an enormous desire to sing in Italian. When I did I was transported to another world. I was untouchable the moment I opened my mouth and sang the first note. I was never one to sit idly by and watch the world move on without me. If there was something I wanted to do, I did it. It didn't matter to me that there wasn't a huge market for Italian cover tunes. I found songs that spoke to me and I recorded them with passion. Life was nothing without passion.

The next year, 2012, I joined The Recording Academy as a voting member. That meant that I got to play a role in deciding who won a Grammy Award. I made so many musician friends from all over the world, it was surreal. One day I'm listening to criminal clients tell me how the police screwed them, the next day I'm voting on whether Justin Bieber should take home a Grammy.

In 2013 I went to the Grammy Awards ceremony at the Staples Center in Los Angeles for the first time. That night, I got a very small taste of what it was like to be part of celebrity culture. I was wide-eyed at this exclusive event and the sheer swankiness of it all. Still, I was ready to return to real life after the weekend. I'd had enough of the paparazzi and security guards with those little wires in their ears. Of course, as soon as the plane touched down in Boston's dreary, midwinter landscape I was ready to go back to Los Angeles for the Grammys the next year. Los Angeles has an allure that cannot be adequately described.

The next year, 2014, Mark and I returned to the Grammy Awards ceremony and I had the thrill of my life: I got to walk on the red carpet. I stepped into the tent illuminated by extravagant chandeliers with reporters buzzing around interviewing musicians and recording artists. Me. On the red carpet. At the Grammy Awards. When I was a little girl singing in front of the mirror with my hairbrush as my microphone, if someone had said that one day I'd be on the red carpet at the Grammys, I never would have believed it. I soaked up every second I spent in that tent and vowed that I would return someday as a nominee.

By now, I was making a name for myself locally through my various gigs, and I also performed at many of my hometown's events. I began to develop a decent following of fans and was offered a variety of performance opportunities. At last, my career was taking shape. All the years of hard work were paying off.

In 2013, besides going to Grammys for the first time, I attended Berklee College of Music's Umbria Jazz Clinics in Perugia, Italy. It was an unequivocally life-changing experience for me. I saw true talent in its raw form and the enthusiasm of students just beginning their musical journeys. I learned a lot about people that summer.

During the Berklee program, I performed in a few jams at Trottamundo, a jazz club in the historical heart of the small city, and onstage at the Umbria Jazz Festival, where I performed a small solo and also sang as part of a choir. I met a young woman named Ilaria at the program and we became fast friends. We were in the same ensemble class and we performed onstage at the festival in a duet of "Summertime" with our class. We also sang a duet of "At Last" at Trottamundo during one of the open mic jam sessions held throughout the festival.

I had performed in Boston many times, but something about the energy of the Umbria Jazz Festival was different. As I reveled in the culture and the music, I realized there was so much more to life than I had ever imagined. Meeting new friends from various parts of the world and bonding over love of music was something I hadn't experienced before.

It's true, I had played with many amazing professional musicians—amazingly talented and experienced artists in the Boston music scene—but the students in Italy were different. Their very essences exuded a pure love of music. I felt their powerful desire and tremendous musical energy. Many of them wanted badly to study at Berklee College of Music in Boston but most couldn't afford to realize their musical dreams that way. And here I was, an American completing the program in Perugia as a bonus and simply because I wanted a different musical experience. I could afford to go to the summer program whenever I wanted to, while for many others the program was a once-in-a-lifetime chance. I realized how lucky I was to live where I did, with the many musical opportunities that I had, and to have the money to record CDs and travel anywhere I wanted. I lived just a few miles from the main Berklee campus in Boston and I could listen to the raw talent of students from around the world, alongside phenomenal teachers and artists, whenever I pleased. I could hop in the car and be at Birdland in New York City in four hours to hear some of the finest jazz musicians in the world. I was fortunate, to say the least.

I performed one evening at Trottamundo with a house band, as well as with a fellow student on saxophone. He was very young and somewhat of a beginner, but the way he played the notes with great passion told me all I needed to know about why I was there in the first place.

There are no coincidences in life. I needed this entire musical experience to help me understand who I was deep inside, to stir my soul and give me the strength I would need to regain my voice the following year when I lay in a hospital bed filled with despair and only a glimmer of hope for my future. When I sang onstage in that tiny Italian jazz club, I sang from my heart. Every emotion inside of me poured out when I sang "My Funny Valentine." My voice was powerful. It was me. I had been opened spiritually and set on a path. I was able to see the big picture and where exactly that path was to lead me.

I reflected on all of this from my bed in the ICU at Mass General. I knew that returning to Umbria Jazz again was an incredibly lofty goal, especially given the state I was in, but I couldn't give up on it. I had to return to being that person again. I couldn't just lie there and allow life to pass me by. My friend Ilaria was in Italy, and I couldn't bear the thought of never seeing her again. It seemed impossible, but there had to be a way. I didn't know how difficult the road was going to be, but I knew one thing for certain: I had to move from this bedridden, half-paralyzed state to getting on an airplane and singing at an international jazz festival in Europe the next year.

Chapter Six

A S I LAY IN MY ICU bed that first week, I tried to sing. I wanted to see if I could still do it. I was weak, but maybe I could muster up the energy to hit a few notes.

Anytime I was sick and had an upcoming show, I'd sing the first verse of "At Last." I'd crack out a version of that song to reassure myself. That's how I always knew my voice was going to be okay. It became a test of sorts. I knew the song so perfectly I could sing it in my sleep. The melody was etched into my brain from years of performing it at almost every gig. If I could sing my signature song, I was going to be fine.

"At laaaaast..." I wailed.

I couldn't do it! It was a tone-deaf scream. I knew what the melody was supposed to sound like, but my body just couldn't do it. I couldn't even match the pitch of the first few notes. Maybe I wasn't going to be okay after all.

I began to cry. My singing voice was my lifeblood. I thought back to the times when I had sung a solo in my high school choir and the many times my friends and I haunted the now-defunct Weylu's Chinese Restaurant and sang karaoke in their lounge. I recalled the many retreats to my parents' basement to sing along with my karaoke machine for hours, the home recordings I made for my friends, and the vocal coaching I did for a few students in the 1990s. I remembered the many nights I performed with the Al Vega Trio, recorded CDs in the studio, and sang at the Umbria Jazz Festival. Everything was gone.

I flip-flopped back and forth between feeling like a warrior to feeling sorry for myself. Until that point it had been easy for me to imagine being normal again because I hadn't attempted to move beyond lifting my good arm in bed. But reality was creeping in. All of my vocal training and practice for the last thirty years had been replaced with a sound that was something like fingernails screeching across a chalkboard.

Life had really thrown me a one heck of a curveball and there seemed to be nothing I could do about it. I had never thought, even for a millisecond, that my singing ability could vanish into thin air without any warning.

Sure, I'd read horrific stories in the news — stories about people, top athletes even, who had suffered tragic accidents and become paralyzed. Their careers were finished in a flash. But something like that would never happen to *me*. Not *me*. I never worried about it. I didn't gamble with my health or take needless safety risks. I didn't ski down treacherous slopes at 100 miles an hour, or do things like carelessly jump headfirst into the shallow end of a swimming pool. I never thought about what would happen if I were to suddenly become paralyzed for no discernible reason. Who does?

A few friends stopped in to see me in the ICU during the next few days. My friend Kim and her husband, Rich, visited. Kim was in shock, too, as she had seen me the night before the stroke and I had been fine. We had laughed together, sipping limoncello and dangling our feet in my swimming pool. I'll never forget the look on their faces when they first saw me. They tried to be upbeat, but it was impossible. This was an undeniably horrible situation. I said to Kim in a calm voice, "I don't care if my body is permanently paralyzed, as long as I can still sing."

For days, I lay in that ICU, just existing, unable to move the left side of my body. The days in the hospital were monotonous and painful as I kept thinking of more things that had been taken from me. It was a relentless, constant, pitiful feeling. It was like a thousand knives stabbing me in the heart. My own body had betrayed me. Maybe I needed to accept that the performing chapter of my life was over, that I had to focus on learning to live life in a wheelchair and independently using the toilet again.

Another friend, Michelle, came to see me in ICU. Michelle is an opera singer, a music teacher, and the mother of my six-year-old godson, Lucca. We've been friends since grade school, we traveled to Disneyworld together to sing in our high school choir competition, she sang at my wedding, and we went to London together a couple of years before. She even helped me out by working at my law practice as a paralegal. We used to joke about what we'd be like in our elderly years. We would become two old ladies sitting on a couch, laughing about the crazy things we'd done in our lifetimes. Now I was living those years — at forty-two. And I certainly wasn't laughing about it.

I tried to sing for Michelle, but I just couldn't do it. She knew my singing voice was gone. After she left, I thought of Al Vega again. He would never have put up with this nonsense. He would have insisted he could get up, book musicians, and do a jazz gig in the hospital waiting room. He would figure out how to get himself out of the hospital and back on stage in no time. And that's exactly what I had to do.

I had to reclaim my life before it slipped away.

After the life-changing experience of Umbria Jazz in 2013, I knew I had to return to Italy. I felt like I belonged there. I wanted to see Ilaria again. I had never been to Venice. So, in January 2014, my friend Rosanna and I traveled to Italy for a short visit. We visited Ilaria at her home in Venice and she was excited to see me. Venice took my breath away — gondolas that floated timelessly in the lagoons, art and architecture that uplifted my soul. I couldn't wait to visit more places like Venice, to see more of what life had to offer.

Rosanna and I planned to visit another Italian friend, in Lucca, and then go on to Florence. We stayed in Pisa as it was easy to access both cities from there. But Rosanna had to leave unexpectedly and return home, which meant I would stay in Pisa alone and finish the trip solo. I had never traveled alone internationally before, but I wasn't afraid. I felt free! I explored the city, marveled at the

Leaning Tower, took the train to Lucca and Rome, had a layover in Switzerland on the way home, and enjoyed every minute of it.

Mark bought me a handheld music recorder for Christmas just a few weeks before the trip, and I had it with me in Italy. I never knew when the occasion to sing would arise and I wanted to always be prepared. That recorder would end up capturing one of the last times I had my singing voice. Was it to remind me of what my voice could return to again? I'll never know. But I'm glad I brought it. I recorded an *a cappella* rendition of "At Last" with Ilaria in Venice and a jazz version of "Summertime" on a street corner in Pisa. The recording was just voice and one of my friends playing saxophone, the same young Italian student who had performed "My Funny Valentine" with me in the Perugia jazz club. The combination of voice and saxophone sounded as smooth as silk. That simple recording filled my soul with joy. It wasn't Grammy-worthy material, especially with the sound of the local trash collection truck in the background, but the short recording captured my love for singing. When I returned to the States I had the recording professionally engineered and I made it available on SoundCloud. It would become one of my most treasured recordings.

Attending Berklee Umbria Jazz in 2013 was an inspiration to me musically and spiritually. When the program was over and I was back home in the United States I could truly understand what was musically important. It wasn't about how much money I made from selling CDs, performing at gigs, or how wide my vocal range was. It was my passion for music that mattered. Everything else would fall into place. I decided to scale back on law and pursue music as a career, putting all of my efforts into it. I'd had enough of straddling the line between lawyer and musician.

On my return from Italy I enrolled in the Berklee Umbria Jazz Clinics again, for the summer of 2014. I spent several months preparing, practicing new songs, looking forward to seeing friends I'd made the previous year. I was eager to learn as much as I could about vocal technique and music theory because I planned to apply to the master's program at Berklee the following year to further my musical knowledge.

Not everyone is lucky enough to experience music the way I did. I had been born with a gift and my path was illuminated by musical desire. I only had to take my vocal abilities to the farthest limits within my reach. Anything less was unacceptable.

Until now, while singing was a way I bared my soul, I mostly sang other people's songs. I had written one short tune with a retro feel, but it lacked the depth I wanted.

Now, I began writing original material. I was recording a new CD of original, retro-inspired music. And I loved every second of it. Inspired by thoughts of Italy and of Berklee Umbria Jazz the previous summer, how small the world really was, and how as individuals we are all connected on a spiritual level, I could express myself through music in a way I'd never been able to. I could write for hours.

Once I saw the truth in music and how it could take me to the highest high or the lowest low, I couldn't go back to a shallow musical existence. I wrote about love and trust, faith and longing, all sorts of emotions common to us all. Mostly I wrote from an outsider's perspective looking in, but my feelings were sincere as I wrote and when I sang.

Music can awaken your soul. And once it has been awakened, your entire outlook changes. The little things stay little. Waiting in line at the bank isn't going to kill you.

The traffic will pass.

My friendship with Ilaria is a perfect example of how spirituality and music work together to reveal the essence, or soul, of a person. When we first met, I knew very little about Ilaria, yet I was so comfortable with her I felt like she could have been the sister I never had. When I returned to Venice the following winter, I learned that Ilaria shared my sense of spirituality. We shared beliefs and, above all, we shared a fervent passion for music. When I moved to rehab after ICU, Ilaria messaged me every single day in an effort to lift my spirits. She told me I would recover. She talked me out of my doubts when I had them. She treated me like the old Valerie, the woman I so desperately needed to be reminded about. And she did all of this from her computer, many thousands of miles away.

Chapter Seven

A LMOST AN ENTIRE WEEK HAD passed since the stroke and I was still seeing double.

Everything in my world was detected through sound because of my double vision and because I constantly had to squint one eye. It was easier to keep both eyes shut. Finally, the ICU nurses made a gauze eye patch for me and taped it to my eyeglasses so I could move the patch to either eye and see singularly.

My hearing was operating on overdrive. Everything was extremely loud. All day the harsh sounds of the nurses' ringing cell phones plagued me. Their ringtones sounded like they were connected to a loudspeaker in my brain. Anxious, I'd shout, "What's going on? What's happening?" every time I heard those excruciatingly loud ringtones. I was terrified the sound I was hearing signaled some new problem, or that I was having another stroke.

And I was dizzy. The dizziness was so bad that only a sedative could calm me down enough to allow me to sleep. I could only sleep at night, after a dose of Ativan delivered by IV. Before the stroke, I loved napping. I could sleep on a picket fence at any time of day. Now, even the slightest bob of my head as I drifted off to sleep sent me spinning for hours.

I also lost the ability to dream. Until then, I'd had extremely intricate dreams and I usually remembered them well. When my grandmother was alive, we'd talk about our dreams—she was also interested in deciphering meanings in dreams. Growing up, I liked to read her dream interpretation books, and as an adult I frequently looked up the meanings of my dreams. I'd recalled my dreams every night for as long as I could remember. They were like a movie playing itself out. The stories were fragmented, disjointed and full of symbolism. I felt fortunate to have such vivid dreams and to be able to recall them the next morning. Now I had none. I went to sleep and woke up.

Everything in between was blank. How much more was there to lose?

This was my new schedule: I woke at four a.m., after a dreamless few hours of drug-induced sleep. When I opened my eyes, the dizziness was there, greeting me for yet another fun-filled day of mere "existence" as I stared straight ahead with one eye squinted while the room spun around me.

And every time I closed my eyes the dizziness was there with a vengeance, just waiting to pounce on my brain. Since I couldn't move from the bed, I couldn't even use the restroom. I was being given so much fluid by IV that I had to pee every five seconds, which required yelling for the nurses to bring a bedpan and help me. I had zero muscle control. Any hesitation on the nurses' part and I would have to lie there in wet sheets until the nurses came to clean me up. I couldn't think of anything more humiliating. Using the bedpan wasn't easy either. I was so violently dizzy that the movement of swinging my ass from side to side to get me onto the bedpan itself was absolutely horrid. I held onto the bed rail with my right hand to do this, and just the rolling motion of my body made the dizziness so much more intense that I cried out every time. "Ahhh…dizzy!…Oh my God….I can't do this!" as if shouting those words somehow helped my situation. It didn't.

I knew I needed to mold my body and mind into a recovery machine, but the dizziness held me back, leaving me with no idea how I could accomplish that. But there had to be a way! Wallowing in self-pity was getting me nowhere. When would all this be over? What did I do to deserve this? Was God punishing me? Surely, there had to be a reason.

My parents suffered, too. The last thing they'd ever expected was to see their daughter suffer a stroke at forty-two. "I should be trading places with you," my father remarked one day in my ICU room. "You don't belong here. I do."

The entire nursing staff was so good to me. They treated me like the most important person on earth and made me feel like I truly mattered. Danielle, one of the nurses, always talked to me, calming me in the dizzy moments and giving me hope that things would improve.

"Will I ever be normal again?" I asked Danielle every day.

"You will be," Danielle would say, giving me her kind, caring smile. "This is only a blip on the radar."

Hmmm. A blip on the radar. It sounded good. I'd go with that. I clutched onto that simple phrase as if it were a lifeboat and I was on the Titanic.

Lying in that bed, I imagined myself in regular settings, places I'd been before this happened. I reviewed holidays spent with my family, going to church, and ordinary things, like shopping at the mall. In this fantasy world I could go to anytime I wanted, I wasn't paralyzed. I lived in my imagination. And just maybe, if I visualized myself recovered, it might happen.

And then something did happen. I swallowed a sip of water when my nurse brought a cup of water to my bedside. I could swallow! It was minimal, and droplets of water cascaded down my chin from the left side of my mouth, but my ability to swallow had come back! I couldn't move my left side, I had to close one eye to see, I was perpetually dizzy, and I had lost my singing ability, but I could swallow water. In that tiny act lived a glimmer of hope that I might one day resume my life as it was before the stroke.

My medical team was called in. From that day on, I started drinking water regularly, provided I had a straw and there was someone to hold the cup close to my mouth. After that, cautiously, the medical team signed off on allowing me to start eating again, soft foods I could easily swallow. I was as excited as a kid on Christmas morning every time the food service staff entered my room with the breakfast tray. I ordered pancakes for my first meal. Hospital pancakes with syrup tasted better than a filet mignon personally cooked by Wolfgang Puck! Granted, I had to be fed, which was as humiliating as the bedpan situation, but I didn't care. I was starving for real food. In the afternoons and evenings, my mother usually fed me, just as she had done when I was a baby, complete with a bib.

The shock of all of this was enormous to my husband. Mark's eyes were red and teary all the time. He didn't talk much. He slept in my ICU room every night in a reclining chair behind my bed. I often called out for him just to make sure he was still in my room because I was afraid to be alone, especially since I couldn't move and was barely able to see.

When Mark and I married in 2007, neither of us could have expected we'd have to endure something like this. Eating with a bib around my neck? Maybe if I were a hundred years old. But at forty-two? I'm sure the thought of our living like this for the rest of our lives worried Mark. At this rate it looked like he would be relegated to a life of living alone and visiting me every day in some long-term-care nursing facility unable to see straight or move much no less take care of myself for even the most basic of bodily functions. Mark would become my full-time caretaker during my recovery.

My prospects looked bleak. Despite Dr. Singhal's optimism about my coming out of this, no one really knew if I would ever recover or if I was fated to spend the rest of my life in a nursing home. Stroke recovery can't be predicted. Everyone recovers at their own pace and to varying degrees. Some people don't recover at all. I couldn't afford NOT to recover by anything less than a hundred percent, or at least I had to try for it.

When Mark told my friend Annette about the stroke, she raced to visit me in the ICU. She brought me a balloon with a smiley face on it. I stared at that balloon all day, every day. Sometimes it would sway from side to side or bounce up and down. It became a way for me to pass the hours while taking my mind off the constant dizziness. Annette was visiting me when a lab technician came in to draw my blood. "I'm Patience," she said, introducing herself. Annette and I looked at each other. It was clear that we both thought the presence of this woman in my room was no coincidence. What were the chances of someone named Patience being brought to me so early in my stroke battle? Maybe this was some sort of spiritual sign? I was surely going to need a lot of patience. How puzzling it all was. God punished me for some reason with this stroke and then asked me to have patience?

Patience, the lab tech, told me that God would take care of everything and I was going to be okay, and she pricked me with a needle and drew my blood. There was something about her presence and tone that seemed odd. She spoke matter-of-factly in a Haitian accent, like she *knew* God. She radiated a feeling of serenity and assurance. I wanted to know God too. I was tired of feeling empty inside. At first, I thought these feelings were side effects of the drugs I was taking to treat the stroke. But as Patience spoke, Annette and I were transfixed by her tone, by the certainty of her words. I never saw Patience again after that day. It was as if she came to me just to relay a message from God that I was going to be okay. Maybe her purpose was to restore the faith in Him that I needed so desperately during those dark days and to remind me of the importance of patience. Maybe my soul's purpose was to conquer this stroke and help others overcome their adversities. I realized that having the stroke wasn't a punishment. I was alive for a reason. God was *saving* my life and giving me a second chance.

Day after day, nursing staff scurried in and out of my room. I always wanted to know what was going on. What was that beeping sound? Why was that cell phone ringing? They deserve a medal for the way they tended to me. Danielle was always kind, always showing me compassion. "This is going to be a marathon, you know, not a sprint," she explained gently. A marathon? I wanted to recover as fast as possible. My lack of patience was in full swing, which is why I believe a nurse named "Patience" was sent to draw my blood one day. I like to think it was a spiritual reminder. I needed one.

Healing is a choice. I had to decide if I wanted to live like this forever. How could I continue to just exist like this? What about all the barbecues, the traveling, and, of course, the singing? Those things were not going to magically return on their own. My life until now had been pretty easy. When I wanted something, I went after it and I usually got it. But I had never been this challenged before. I knew I had to do the work to get my life back. It would take sheer determination and a huge amount of effort on a very tough path. But sometimes the only road worth traveling is the hardest one.

Chapter Eight

S EVERAL DAYS HAD PASSED AND I was eating again, soft foods like pancakes and Jell-O, and I was considered out of the woods. Big event! I was transferred from my bed in the ICU into a regular hospital room.

The days were still one gigantic blur, a monotonous cycle of lying in bed, staring straight ahead, and calling for a bedpan every half hour. But my vision was beginning to clear and I could finally open both eyes. I repeatedly explained to the nursing staff that I had to be better in a few days as I was going to Italy soon.

"What a nice goal to have," said one of my nurses.

They knew the stark reality of the situation. I wasn't leaving the hospital anytime soon. It was going to be a long time before I visited Italy again, if ever. Never mind singing, I could barely swallow. I had a blood clot in my brain and no left side. I couldn't move my head. I had no singing voice. How I wanted to stay in denial and think I could fly to Italy, sing, and ask my friends to carry me on a special bed to the school every day. My trip to Italy was the last bit of my old life that refused to surrender.

Mark made the cancellation phone call to Berklee Umbria Jazz. Clara, my friend in the front office, couldn't believe it when he told her what happened to me. We had met the year before and she'd been looking forward to seeing me at the summer program in just a few weeks. She told Mark to send me her best wishes for recovery.

"I did it," Mark told me sadly, after he made the call. He took my hand and squeezed it, but I couldn't squeeze back. There was no consolation possible. I held onto the Berklee in Italy as a last chance, a last scrap of hope that I was the same woman I'd been before that horrible day in June. Now it was official; my old life was completely gone, and along with it, all of my dreams and musical aspirations. There was nothing left to look forward to. My life consisted of lying in my hospital bed, staring straight ahead. There was no bottom to my grief.

Soon, something miraculous happened. Right in that hospital bed, my hips moved, both of them. I raised them up off the bed like I was in some 1980s aerobics video. I was moving! Mark stepped back for a better look. "Look at you!" he cried.

Granted, it was a miniscule amount of movement, but it was movement nonetheless. Mark bent to whisper in my ear. "You're going to get out of here. It's going to happen."

All that day I proceeded to show off my new hip-moving feats to everyone who visited me. "Look!" I'd exclaim. "I can move my hips!" And then I'd show them.

Patience, right?

Within days, a doctor came to see me with some good news. "You're going to be transferred to Spaulding Rehabilitation Hospital in Charlestown in a few days," she said. "You're ready."

Rehab! I was getting out of the hospital! I was filled with questions. What would I do there? Would I walk on the treadmill? Lift weights? Would Spaulding be able to give me my life back?

That day, I began to have more hope for my future. I still couldn't see without that eye patch stopping the double vision. I was half-paralyzed, I was dizzy, I could barely swallow, and I had a blood clot in my brain stem. But I could move my hips in my hospital bed, and nothing was going to stand in the way of my recovery. Nothing.

Spaulding Rehabilitation Hospital in Boston has a stellar reputation as one of the best rehab facilities in the country. The April 2013 Boston Marathon bombing survivors were treated there. They were frequently on the TV news, shown doing activities like driving and traveling. Maybe Spaulding could help me the way it helped them. Surely, Spaulding could put me back together too.

The day before I was transferred there, I woke up seeing normally again.

I couldn't believe it. I didn't need the eye patch! How liberating it was to not need that patch. I could swallow again, move my hips, *and* I could see clearly. I was still unable to move my left side and I was dizzy, but it was a start.

Before I was discharged from the hospital, I was given a final CT scan of my brain to be sure I wouldn't have another stroke. I like to think of it as Mass General's parting gift to me. Everything looked good enough to Dr. Singhal and he gave me the green light.

Paramedics transferred me from my hospital bed to a stretcher for the ambulance ride. Every movement was torture. I was a slave to the dizziness and there was nothing I could do to stop it. Finally, I was loaded onto the ambulance, with a neck brace so that I wouldn't move around if we experienced a few bumps.

The elevator ride to the garage bay was an adventure. Every time the stretcher was wheeled down the hall or to an elevator, I cringed from the pain and the spinning. But I managed to do it. The ambulance then transported me from MGH to Spaulding Rehab in the Charlestown area, my new home for a while. I had no idea how long I'd be at Spaulding, and I didn't care. All I could think about was what sort of rehab activities I could do if given the chance. I couldn't see beyond that and, frankly, I didn't want to go home yet. I knew I was in no position to be at home without nurses. Spaulding was swanky and new, and filled with nurses and doctors. I would be safe there.

Spaulding was like the Ritz-Carlton of rehabs. Within an hour I was settled into a private room overlooking Boston Harbor. It was large and clean, and I was given a therapy binder to chart my progress.

All day that first day at Spaulding, I lay in bed, dizzy as hell. I couldn't turn my head an inch. When my family visited they had to position their chairs at the foot of my bed so I could see them.

Therapy began first thing the next morning. A young woman

named Alex greeted me in my room. "Good morning," she said. "Are you ready to take your first steps?"

Alex was a petite young woman who was very enthusiastic about her job. She was happy, positive, brimming with a wide smile, and she had an attitude of endless patience. Every day, I smelled coffee on her breath and I thought about how "normal" her life was. I could just see it. She got up, got dressed, made coffee, and headed to Spaulding for a day of work. What I wouldn't have given to have a life like that. To actually be able to do those "insignificant" things in life that are so easily taken for granted. Imagine what it would be like to be able to go to a coffee shop, wait in line, and hand over cash to the clerk with my fingers. Could Alex help me do those things again? I was hopeful. Did she say I would actually be *walking*? I couldn't believe it. I had already almost forgotten what it felt like.

I held Alex's arm and propped myself up on the bed with my right hand. It was the first time I was able to do anything except stare straight ahead. "That's it, that's it," said Alex, gently guiding me with a hand on my back. I sat for a few moments as the room spun. It was horribly disorienting. Alex stood by me, giving me her presence and not pressuring me to make another move, not yet anyway.

"Okay," she said, finally. "I want you to try to get off this bed. Do you think you can do it?" She kept one hand on my back and put her other hand on my left shoulder to help guide me.

"Let's go," I said. I wanted to be brave. I wanted to do this more than anything.

First, I swung my right leg to the left, and then, with my right hand, I manually moved my left leg so that both of my legs hung over the edge of the bed. Everything was spinning wildly around me.

"This is great," said Alex. "You're doing great." "I'm spinning," I said. "Dizzy."

"You're okay," she assured me.

Alex kept a hand on my back while she pressed a button on the bed control and lowered the bed. I loved the sound of that machine! I was moving down; I was getting out of bed!

"You're going to transfer to a wheelchair," Alex said.

I noticed the wheelchair for the first time. "Are you sure I can do this? What if I fall?"

"I'm right here," Alex said. "You won't fall."

Never taking a hand off me, Alex pulled the wheelchair closer and set the brake at the back of it. Then she stood and gently guided me to standing just long enough to be able to ease down into the chair with her support. She wasn't much bigger than me, but she was steady and she was strong.

I wanted to cry. I was out of the bed and in the chair!

"You did it," said Alex. She clapped her hands and gave me a big smile. "Okay, now. Get ready to go."

Alex had been crouched in front of me, making sure my feet were securely set in the footrests and that I was generally alright. Now she stood and went behind the wheelchair and put her hands on the two handholds to steer me.

I was still a bit teary-eyed, wiping at both my eyes with my right hand. "I'm ready," I managed to say. "Let's go."

Alex wheeled me out of the room and into the hallway, which was wide and empty. It felt strange to be in motion, and I was glad she walked very slowly, probably only a foot or so at a time, though it felt strangely fast. "How're you doing?" she asked, bending a little closer as she slowed the chair to a stop. I told her I was fine, and I was, even though I could hardly focus, and the dizziness was unrelenting.

Alex parked the wheelchair with the brake at the back wheels and came around in front of me. She put her hands on her hips and grinned. "Looking good!"

I tried to smile, but there was no way. It was all I could do to sit there with all the spinning.

"Okay, now," she said. "You're going to stand up. I'm right here, don't worry. The chair won't move and you can always sit down if you need to. And there's a railing along the hallway, see? Right here." She patted it with her free hand.

I couldn't quite make out the railing, but I knew where the

wall was and I understood what she meant. I knew, too, that I had a working right side, and I would rely on that for help as well.

Very slowly, I stood up from the wheelchair. Alex stayed by my right side, steadying me with an arm around my waist. My legs felt like jelly. I was wobbly.

"Take the railing," Alex coaxed, helping me reach out for it with my right arm.

It felt great to make contact with that wooden railing. I was up! I was standing on two feet!

"Will you stay with me?" I begged Alex. "Will you be next to me in case I fall?" "I'm right here," she said. "And you're doing it. You're standing!"

My left arm dangled loosely by my side. I felt my left leg but it was an immovable rock. It was one of the most bizarre things I've ever experienced. I couldn't put weight on it, but my right side, so far, was filling in for it just fine if I stayed completely still. Was it really just over a week since I'd gotten paralyzed on my left side? I'd been through so much it felt like an eternity.

I had been a dancer for many years. I'd even won an achievement award at Dance Teacher Training from the Dance Teachers' Club of Boston for teaching a roomful of ballerinas a hip-hop routine to rap music. I had faithfully attended dance classes several times a week for almost eighteen years. In high school I was a choreographer for the show choir, and in college I co-founded Salem State College's Repertory Dance Theater with a few other students. I performed dance solos and choreographed dance routines for public performances. I had the training, I had the discipline, and I had the internal focus from all those years of ballet, jazz, and tap dance classes. I knew what I needed to do to walk again. This was my chance to show what I was made of.

With that thought, staring straight ahead with intense focus, I grabbed Alex's arm tightly as I continued to stand. The hallway on the rehab neurology floor seemed blurry and unreal, like a graphic in a computer game. I let my gaze momentarily rest on the cheerful paintings of colorful flowers on the walls, then move to rest on the square white signs on the door of each patient's room. Everything looked surreal. But at least I was standing. I was crooked, weak, and dizzy, but I was standing. In that moment, the chains that had lain so heavy across my body in the ICU and in the hospital bed were lifted. My journey to reclaiming myself had begun.

Alex was holding me up from behind, her hands on both of my outer thighs. My legs were like Jell-O, and yet they felt terribly stiff.

I moved my right leg forward as I held onto the railing in the hallway with my right hand. Alex placed my left leg in front of me and I took my first step. The hallway was blurry and spinning, and I fought to keep myself from falling over. I had to keep moving. I took another step, and I was done.

Exhausted. After two steps. "That's it?" Alex asked. "That's all I've got," I told her.

She said I'd done great, and she pulled the wheelchair closer so I could ease down into it with her help. Soon after, I was back in the bed, completely wiped out for the rest of the day.

I looked around at my new environment. This place would be my world while I figured out how to get back on my feet. There was a button to ring the nurse for a bedpan or for anything else, there was a glass of water with a straw ready for me the next time I needed a drink from it, and there were no machines with beeping sounds and blinking lights. Joy! I was going to eat dinner that night, granted, with someone's help, but if everything went right it would be something other than orange Jell-O or syrup-sweetened pancakes. I wondered if I could eat a tuna sandwich anytime soon, or a Popsicle, my usual fare. I laughed at the thought. What simple desires. What simple pleasures! I had gotten out of bed and into a wheelchair, moved to the hall, and walked two steps.

I settled back into my bed, which seemed comfortable now, not a death sentence, and I waited, hoping a visitor would come by. My husband? My parents? Other relatives or friends? Even some neighbors had dropped by the hospital on a regular basis, and it meant so much to me. Besides lifting my spirits, all of my visitors had a purpose they weren't even aware of. Each time a nurse or a visitor came into my room, I would look at them with so much envy. I would observe their every move so closely, as if I were studying for an exam. I watched as they walked in my room or used their hands, following their motions with my eyes in an attempt to learn exactly how they did it, how they walked, how they sat, how they washed their hands in the small sink across from my bed. How were they able to move around and why couldn't I? What was it about their bodies that allowed them to effortlessly do these things? I had to find out, so I could move that way again too. There was no way I was going to settle for a life where independence meant that my biggest achievement was regaining the ability to brush my teeth without assistance.

Chapter Nine

THE DAY AFTER I TOOK my first steps in the hallway, Alex appeared after breakfast in my doorway with a big grin. "Ready for the gym?"

I never thought I'd be so happy to be in a wheelchair! I was going somewhere.

Alex wheeled me to the gym for our first physical therapy session. It was an enormous room filled with the latest exercise and therapy equipment, and it was crowded with other patients, fellow disabled people. We paused at the entrance and in a quiet voice, Alex told me these were people with brain injuries, spinal cord injuries, and stroke patients, like me. Most of these people were working with their therapists, seated in wheelchairs or standing with the support of walkers. It looked like one huge training session, everyone working so hard just to do the little things that able-bodied people don't even think about. I saw a woman walking up a short fake staircase, a man throwing a ball few feet away from him, a seated man putting pegs in a board. All of these looked like herculean tasks to me. But I was inspired. If these people could do it, so could I. Most of these patients probably started in a place similar to mine. They might have been hospitalized with a condition that made them unable to move, but look at them now. I wanted to be at their level of progress by tomorrow.

Alex hooked up my wheelchair to a specially adapted stationary bicycle, and I started to sob. My eyes were so full I couldn't see, much less pedal. I just couldn't stop crying. Who had I become?

Where was the old me? *This can't be happening!* I said those words over and over in my mind.

"Why the tears?" Alex asked, bending close.

I stopped crying long enough to answer. "I went to my gym just before this happened!"

"I understand," she said.

"No, I mean, I was so physically active my entire life—I was a dancer, I fenced, I was a high-energy vocalist, moving all over the stage. I had a very full life...and now..." I started to cry again.

Around me, people seemed to be happy exercising. I even heard someone nearby laugh with her therapist.

I had to get it together.

Alex crouched beside me, her chin on her folded hands. She was so kind, so ready to just listen and be there for me.

I wiped my eyes with the back of my sleeve and took a deep breath. "Let's do it," I said.

As always, my dizziness was there with me while I tried to work the bicycle machine. I noticed a man not far from me who couldn't walk or talk. He was attached to a harness and taking small steps with the help of his therapist while his wife excitedly snapped pictures. I wondered about them, what sort of wedding they'd had. Had they traveled the world, like Mark and me? I imagined the man coming home from work and sitting down to dinner with his wife and kids. And here he was now, walking in a harness and making moaning sounds. And she was thrilled. He looked proud and happy himself, displaying his achievements in the gym.

That day I learned something critical. That couple showed me that any obstacle could be overcome. Tragedy could turn into triumph. That couple also showed me there are people who take their wedding vows seriously and stick by the ones they love, in sickness and in health. People like this man's wife. People like my husband, Mark.

After a few minutes, I regained my composure enough to push both bicycle pedals using only my right leg to propel the wheel. As I watched the digital screen attached to the bicycle, I noticed that my left leg was not that much weaker than my right after all, at least according to the percentages reflected on the screen. I had a chance. Maybe my muscles remembered the hundreds of hours they put into the elliptical machine, or the years of dance training? Maybe they just needed to be coaxed a little, pushed to do what they could do. Maybe I wasn't as paralyzed as I thought I was.

Alex was wonderfully patient with me, but it could be hard to watch her. She could do anything she wanted. As the days and weeks went on she'd ask me how my weekend was and tell me about hers, maybe there had been a visit from her family or a special outing she'd made with a friend. I had the feeling she was trying to bring some sense of normalcy back into my life, which is exactly what I needed. There *was* life beyond these walls! But let's face it. My weekends were nothing more than getting a few visitors and staring straight ahead. I might have gone down the hallway and I might have gone into the gym, but I didn't go anywhere besides Spaulding Rehab. Ten minutes of slow pedaling in the gym left me exhausted. After crying for most of that PT session, I had to struggle to regain my composure. I couldn't bear to become known as the resident crier of Spaulding Rehab, the one with frequent bouts of self-pity and excruciating longing for her pre-stroke way of life. And I wanted to fight this and win.

Daily occupational therapy started soon after I arrived at Spaulding, and a young woman named Ari was my therapist. Ari was friendly and compassionate, and she helped me learn to navigate the dailies with my limp left hand and arm, as well as with relearning how to do my personal care. I looked forward to my time with her as there was always something new to be learned.

During the first week of therapy Ari wheeled me into my bathroom for a practice session on how to take a shower and use the toilet. I hadn't seen the inside of a bathroom in a long time. As she wheeled me inside, I saw the toilet, the sink, the three-walled shower with its plastic chair inside, and the paper towel dispenser on the wall. Ari held me in place as I slowly stood up and with the strength of my right side transferred myself onto the plastic shower chair, just as I had done when I stood in the hallway with Alex and grabbed onto the wooden railing. I held onto the bar in the shower and flopped into the plastic chair, thoroughly exhausted.

"You did it," said Ari, ever optimistic.

Ari kept encouraging me, verbally congratulating my every achievement, even if it was something as miniscule as getting myself from the wheelchair onto the shower chair. Each time I accomplished something by myself Ari was quick to cheer me on about my progress. Ari's smile was genuine. She truly wanted to see me succeed in all of our therapeutic activities, which I treated somewhat like a game. Winning was the only option. She wheeled me to the gym, to the games area. There was every game I grew up with — Connect 4, Operation, Fiddlesticks. I played these games by feeling for the plastic pieces set on the table, while looking straight ahead. I used my right hand to put the round pieces through the slots of Connect 4 and put the Operation game's patient's organs back in his body before the timer went off. I had no opponent besides myself, and Ari was my cheerleading section.

Shower practice was a different situation. There, I had to do everything seated, and there were added challenges caused by soap and water. When I attempted to shave my legs, for example, although I managed to manually put my left leg across my right one, it slid down every few seconds. I refused to resemble a gorilla and there were days I had to dress in shorts for therapy. To get myself up from the wheelchair and onto the shower chair, I held onto the bathroom bar with Ari steadying me so I wouldn't fall. And all of the time I had to continue looking straight ahead. I couldn't turn my head an inch.

Next on my daily agenda were speech therapy sessions. Initially, I didn't know what a speech therapist really did. Did they show people how to speak again? How was this done? I could speak, though my words were slightly slurred and my tone was high-pitched. What could these speech therapists teach me to make this go away? All I knew about speech therapy was what I learned in elementary school, when a speech therapist who looked about a hundred years old took a few students out of my classroom for an hour or so. The students came back with tales of playing fun games and making instant pudding in a Styrofoam cup. The speech room was filled with toys, and soon every kid at school wanted to be called in for speech therapy. Eventually, one by one my entire class was allowed to have one speech therapy session, which seemed to consist of making instant pistachio pudding. That was my only prior experience with speech therapy.

I did a little research online and learned that, besides helping correct articulation disorders and impairments, speech therapy could also assess cognitive deficits. Ah-ha! So that was why I was in speech therapy! They wanted to make sure I hadn't lost my mind.

My speech therapist, Carla, was a pleasant, polite young woman who administered cognitive assessments of all different kinds. In one I had to name all the animals I could think of that began with the letter A. Aardvark, antelope....and so on. In another I had to memorize places, names, and fictional fact patterns, and then be tested. I had to balance a checkbook, tell time by reading an analog clock, read simple passages and count all of the conjunctions (and, but, if). In one exercise I had to count backwards by intervals of four.

But the cognitive test I liked the least was the one where I had to devise a logical plan for doing errands. I had to make a map from a list of daily errands and put them in order. I had news for Carla. I never, ever did things in a rational order. Having no children meant I could do anything whenever I felt like it. If I wanted to go to the mall, I cut my errands short and did them the next day or the next week. If I wanted a haircut or a manicure — guess what? I didn't go grocery shopping. Looking good was more important than buying milk if I could get an appointment at the salon. It was the way I operated and it worked for me. I went to college for seven years after high school, earned two degrees, owned a law practice, and made two CDs. Did I really care about pretending to go to the dry cleaners and bank in some kind of strict order? No!

I thought clearly. I had no trouble with memory. I believed, if anything, that the stroke had made my mental faculties stronger. I spent hours on my back remembering my life as it was before the stroke. Besides that, my memory was getting sharper every time I had to prove my mental abilities to Carla with those tests.

The dizziness I experienced all day every day presented the real challenge to performing Carla's cognitive tests. I just wanted the room to stop spinning. Physical and occupational therapies were easier because I could daydream and imagine myself somewhere else when I was moving around. There was no logic to apply to how I was going to shave my legs without drawing blood, it was all about motor skills and being patient. In speech therapy I had to prove what my mind could do while the room was spinning.

I liked Carla, but if I had two operational legs, I would have walked out the door on my first day of speech therapy, when she asked me to make a list of pretend errands that I'd never do. I would never go to a candy store, then buy a lamp, then go to a bakery, and then have lunch with friends all in one morning. Heck, I would never go buy a lamp unless it was a vintage reproduction piece I special-ordered from a dealer after searching online for weeks. Real life was not represented by these tests, that was for sure. But I was a captive audience—I was lying on a bed or sitting in a wheelchair in rehab, with an uncertain fate. I had to participate if I ever wanted to get out of here.

To make it worse, speech therapy presented another challenge to contend with. In part, Carla was there to judge my cognitive abilities and I wanted to show her I was fine mentally. But sometimes I made mistakes.

I work quickly, I always have. Sometimes it's an advantage, sometimes it's not. I lost a spelling bee in third grade because I reversed two letters in a word I hands-down knew how to spell: I spelled "maybe" m-a-b-y-e. I misspelled the word because I was going too fast! I lost the bee. In speech therapy, some of my mistakes were because of my habit of hurrying, but Carla didn't know that. To her I was just another stroke patient. A very disabled stroke patient.

Speech therapy maddened me. I couldn't believe they got paid for playing games about naming animals and telling me I had to go to the dry cleaners before the bakery, while I was paid to deal with criminals who would not hesitate to somehow hold me responsible for getting caught dealing drugs. What a great gig.

I didn't want to appear unappreciative of Carla, but my patience was more than running thin. I needed to learn to walk and sing again, I didn't want to prove I could balance a checkbook. I knew what time it was. Naming animals wasn't my forte, which was fine; I didn't plan to become a zoologist anytime soon. I felt offended by what I considered tests of my intelligence, but I tried not to let my frustrations show.

When Carla began to sprinkle in some assistance with recovery of my singing voice, I couldn't have been more willing. Any attempt I made to sing resulted in a howl that sounded like an animal in distress. It tore my heart into a million pieces. Carla had no experience with singing, but she practiced scales with me and we worked on breath control. She helped me practice holding notes and controlling the volume of my voice on command. After a few weeks I could at least match the pitch of the notes. It was hoarse, uncomfortably loud, and I often broke out in nervous laughter in the middle of singing a note. Sometimes I cried, which didn't help. My vocal quality was awful but I had to relearn to sing if I had any hope of recovering my musical abilities.

I sat in Carla's office every morning gazing out the window at families with children playing outside on the lawn. I would have given anything to trade places with any of them, even the children. Anything but this existence.

After my speech sessions, it was time to relax in my bed. If I had a visitor in the evening, which was usual — a friend or a neighbor usually stopped in — I studied their moves and tried to duplicate them from my bed. I tried to mimic everything they did. I crossed and uncrossed my legs, back and forth in a scissor-type motion. It was like I was on speed or had a tic. I could move my legs, so I did the move over and over.

In the hospital, I'd asked my nurses every day if I would ever be the way I was before the stroke. No one had the answer. In rehab, I asked the staff the same question. In the beginning, I'd mostly hear, "The goal of therapy is to make you independent." What did "independent" mean to a stroke patient like me? I wasn't going to be satisfied with simply being able to pee by myself. I wasn't content to conform to whatever stroke scale my medical team might measure my performance against. I had to find the key to unlock my own door, and for now, it had gone missing.

Chapter Ten

MARK ARRIVED IN THE LATE afternoon every day for his regular overnight stay with me at rehab. He slept on the pullout couch in my room so I wouldn't have to be alone. "Let's see what came back today!" he'd often say with great enthusiasm. He would examine my left leg and arm and the fingers on my left hand with hopes of any new movement. "That's okay. We can try again tomorrow," he'd say. And he'd often add, "Rome wasn't built in a day!" Mark seemed confident I was going to regain all my movement again, there was no question of it.

One morning, one of the rehab staff members came into my room with an announcement. "You're joining a group today," she said, matter-of-factly. "Stroke patients, like yourself."

Really? "That's great!" I said. I was eager to socialize with other patients and put some normalcy into my mundane existence. Maybe I'd even make a friend.

She pressed the button to lower my bed and down I went. A nurse came in and together they transferred me to my chair. One of them asked if I wanted my hair brushed (I did) or if I needed to use the bathroom, and off we went.

I was on my way to group occupational therapy class, a place I would spend an hour a day, six days per week, with fellow stroke survivors. The class would follow my individual therapy, the nurse told me, which concerned me a little, since I was already exhausted after exercising in the gym and sitting in a wheelchair for two hours. But my interest was piqued. I was curious to meet other stroke survivors.

A big conference-style table sat in the center of the room, and about ten people, most of them in wheelchairs, a few in straight-backed chairs, were lined up around it. Most were older, in their seventies or eighties, maybe even their nineties. I scanned the row of stroke survivors the best I could (I couldn't turn my head because the dizziness worsened) to see if there was anyone even close to my age, and I was glad to see there were a few. Two of them sat in regular chairs. Their faces weren't even drooped. Their voices sounded normal when they introduced themselves. They looked tidy and alert.

And then there was me. Physically, I was a disaster. I have curly medium-long dark hair and there wasn't a day I didn't have a horrendous case of bed head—who wouldn't with all the hours I spent there with no chance of even turning to the side, much less grabbing a hairbrush and taming the wildness. My teeth were unbrushed, I wore no makeup, and I spoke in a weak, high-pitched whine. I sounded like a Muppet on drugs. It sounded like there were marbles in my mouth, as the left side of my face still slightly drooped. I couldn't move my head, and attached to my chair was a metal rest to hold my immovable left arm. My legs were unshaven, and I wore white orthopedic-style sneakers.

We started by introducing ourselves and sometimes even telling our stroke stories. We would introduce ourselves every day, since new patients joined the group all the time. People left the group too, as soon as they could, and it looked like a few would be gone by the end of the week. I learned that some went on to nursing homes after their stay, an event I swore would never happen to me. Even with everything I had been through these last few weeks, being in a nursing home and sitting in a wheelchair wearing a bib and playing Solitaire for hours scared the daylights out of me. Mark had promised to care for me in sickness and in health, I reminded myself. But how far could it go? How long could he hang on?

"I am here because I turned over too fast in bed," I said, when it was my turn to tell my stroke story. A silence fell over the group. If a gasp could have gone around that room, it would have. They were shocked. Or maybe they didn't believe me. It did sound ridiculous, I knew, but I couldn't be making it up. Why would anyone be here if they didn't have to be? I added that I had been super healthy and active, but a wrong neck turn in bed one morning had broken my neck arteries, causing a blood clot in my brain stem and I'd had a stroke.

The other stroke patients described having underlying conditions like high blood pressure, diabetes, weight issues, and plain old age. Some admitted they had let themselves go and thought they had caused their stroke by not having a healthy lifestyle. Everyone listened very gravely to their stories.

Current events was the first activity of the day, a discussion of top news stories.

This turned out to be my only link to the outside world, as I could barely watch TV because of my dizziness and because it was too painful seeing actors portraying life as I used to know it. A staff member would introduce a topic and anyone who wanted to speak would volunteer his or her thoughts. Newbies like me, and a number of the others, just listened. I didn't like the sound of my strange voice, and there was no way I would be able to project across the room.

After current events, the remainder of the class was spent playing a game of one sort or another. Usually, we started with each of us, one by one, rolling — or gently throwing — a ball across the table to another patient. I always used my left hand to throw and catch, though it typically resulted in the ball rolling off the table. I placed my left hand over the ball using my right hand. I had no grip. But I had to engage that arm as much as possible.

In one of the classes, we met Brian, the staff music therapist. Music therapy? I was interested. Brian played guitar and piano and, that first day, he hopped behind a small keyboard to lead us in a game of Name That Tune. *Name That Tune?* He played songs like "Twinkle, Twinkle" and "Hey, Jude," songs I knew from the moment the first notes were played. I debated about whether to keep blurting out the song titles, then I decided I had better stop. Dominating in a rehab game was not the reputation I wanted. I satisfied myself instead with identifying the songs to myself, reassured that I hadn't lost my musical knowledge, just my musical ability. My singing voice might have been damaged, but my mind was active and alive.

Next, Brian led the class in a cup-banging exercise.

For a musician, it is incomprehensible that musical abilities could be wiped out literally overnight. What had happened to me would be like a pianist having both hands chopped off and never again being able to bring their souls to life through touching the piano keys. A musician's worst nightmare had become my reality.

And so, as the stroke survivors group banged their cups, creating an ear-splitting cacophony, I lost it yet again, sobbing right there in class. I was fed up with being in this caged physical state.

Still, there was a musician in the house, as they say, and I wanted to take advantage of it. I asked Brian for private music therapy sessions. He had the ability, I was certain, and his attitude was pleasant and encouraging, so I knew we'd enjoy working together. I wasn't much of a folksy singer, which seemed to be his musical genre, but any musical instruction at all would be a help and I had to start immediately if I wanted my voice back.

Right away, Spaulding Rehab arranged for private vocal sessions in my room with Brian. He accompanied me on guitar while I attempted to sing an Otis Redding song and then an Amy Winehouse song. It helped to practice songs by people who were deceased rather than by people who were thriving in their musical careers. Otis and Amy's lives were cut off too short, which helped me stay grateful. At least I was alive and I still had a glimmer of a chance.

I marveled at Brian's ability to play guitar as he went through the melodies phrase by phrase. I gazed intently as his fingers moved effortlessly across the fret board of his Yamaha while I sang, not caring that I was so dizzy half a song wiped me out. I thanked him profusely every time for this opportunity. If I could learn to walk again while dizzy and unbalanced and with one leg weakened to the point of paralysis, I could surely regain and retrain my singing voice.

Yet doubt is an intrepid foe, and my progress was so infinitesimal there were days I questioned everything. Even if I got my singing voice back, would it ever sound the same? Would it sound effortless and melodious, like water cascading over stones? Would I be able to draw out that purity of tone, that soul-rending beauty of sound?

It's difficult to describe the utter anguish I felt after initially being paralyzed on my left side. My "old" life was always taunting me with happy memories, leading me to believe I still lived that life. It was a double-edged sword. I had to feel normal in order to reclaim my life, but I couldn't do anything I used to do. In ways, I was held in suspended disbelief.

I will always remember what my father said to me on one of those early days in rehab. He understood what had happened and he had no question I could reclaim myself. "Valerie," he said, both of his hands firmly clasping my good arm, "you will recover and you will be an inspiration to a lot of people. I know you. You don't give up on anything."

That sort of unshakeable confidence was what I needed most to quell my doubt. I just needed to find my inner strength. I hoped I could.

Late that night, I had a breakthrough realization. I had to truly accept my situation if I was going to get out of it. And that launched the first big step forward in my recovery.

But just as I was ready to make that big attitude shift, I was side-swiped.

After a stroke, the body becomes very weak. I didn't know this yet. The day after my great insight, when my resolve to get through this and get my body back was strong and clear, I vigorously hurried through my therapies at the gym without taking a break to drink water. I wanted to make the most of it without letting the dizziness derail my progress. I maintained that level of intensity and focus through the next two therapy sessions, occupational therapy individually, and the group occupational therapy class.

After completing my therapies for the day, I attended a class with other patients on my floor to learn about stroke and its causes. As I read the written materials about different types of stroke, I suddenly became nauseous and panicky. Sweat dripped from my brow and my eyes filled with tears. What was happening? Luckily, Mark had come to the class that day and he noticed me losing my composure.

"Wheel me back to my room immediately!" I told him.

Something was very wrong. As Mark wheeled me through the hallway toward my room, I suddenly lost my vision. All I could see was a blinding bright light. It wasn't *the* bright light that people describe seeing in a near-death experience, it was a frightening sheet of white accompanied by a sickening feeling. I screamed for help, and nursing staff rushed to my aid. They quickly transferred me from my chair to my bed and the whole time all I could hear was a loud ringing sound in my ears. What could possibly be next?

I started to tremble.

After a few minutes of lying on my bed, I could see and hear again. Thank God. But I was still terrified. Another stroke would surely destroy any progress I'd made. It seemed like another cruel joke from the Universe.

A CT scan and MRI at the hospital that day — with injected dye so the doctors could get a good look at my vertebral arteries — showed no negative events had occurred. More tests were done. The problem? I was dehydrated from a combination of working hard in therapy and not drinking enough water.

The days and weeks passed, and I could finally transfer from my bed to a wheelchair with the help of only one nurse. Progress. However, someone still had to be with me at all times because I was still so dizzy that I was afraid to be alone, even in my room. My parents traded off with my in-laws, taking turns "babysitting" me. I was chaperoned everywhere I went, which mainly consisted of the hospital cafeteria and courtyard.

I used every opportunity I could to make progress. When I sat in my wheelchair I would push down on my right leg and will my left leg to move. It moved a little at the knee when I was lying in bed. When I sat in the wheelchair, for the most part it was a dead leg in a brace.

Gradually, Alex built me up to walking ten or twenty steps with a cane and brace. To do this, I'd place the cane in front of me and silently chant the word "step." Then I would take a step with my right and then with my left, repeating to myself, "Step one, step two." This is how I learned to walk again.

We worked on balance. I used dance techniques, putting my right hand out as if I was about to launch into a ballet sequence. I'm pretty sure I was the only patient incorporating fluid ballet movements into physical therapy. And it worked. Soon, I excelled at the balance exercises, even doing them while I was dizzy.

To a rational and logical mind, my prior dance training was nothing but a lucky choice of a hobby. To a believer in destiny, my dance training was so much more than that. It was part of my path, one of the many factors that converged in a perfect storm to enable me to reclaim my life.

My debut CD release, "Songbook," ©
2009. Photo by Michelle Manzi-Grasso.
CD cover design by Disc Makers

View from the stage during my solo.
Photo by Foto Fratticioli © 2013.

My second CD release, "The Italian
Project," © 2011, Palma Records. Photo
by Vintage Girl Studios © 2011 and CD
cover design by Williams & Partners.

At the Shalin Liu performace center
in Rockport, Massachusetts, with the
Cape Ann Big Band, December 2013.

At the rehearsal for Chick Singer
Night, a few hours before suffering my
stroke. Photo by Marcia J. Macres.

Performing my solo onstage at the Umbria
Jazz Festival 2013 in Perugia, Italy, with
fellow students in the Berklee College
of Music Umbria Jazz Clinic program.
Photo by Foto Fratticioli © 2013.

With fellow stroke patient Mike Mortimer at Spaulding Rehabilitation Hospital, Charlestown, Massachusetts, in July 2014. Photo by Brian Mortimer.

Learning to play my new cello, September 2014.

Returning home for the first time, July 2014.

Learning to use my left hand at Spaulding Rehabilitation Network Outpatient Center, November 2014.

Early in my journey to recovery, July 2014.

My first singing performance after the stroke. At the Real School of Music in Burlington, Massachusetts, in November 2014.

75

In Massachusetts General Hospital after
falling on my head, December 2014.

Learning to run at Spaulding Rehab
Outpatient Center in April, 2015.

Indoor rock climbing with
Spaulding Rehab, January 2015.

Performing at Chick Singer Night Boston,
June 2015. Photo by Marcia J. Macres.

On the red carpet at the Grammy
Awards, February 2015.

Wearing heels again! With my husband
Mark Samson in October, 2015

Chapter Eleven

I WAS HARDLY EVER ALONE IN rehab, which was exactly what I wanted. Every day, when rush-hour traffic snarled the highways and commuters crowded the streets to make their way home, I would lie in bed eagerly awaiting Mark's arrival, my eyes fixed on the doorway to my room.

A long curtain hung there to give me some privacy without making me feel closed in. With every passing footstep I listened for the sound of Mark's steps. It became a sort of game to guess who was coming to visit based on the sound of their shoes. I knew Mark's choice of footwear and was excited the moment I'd see sneakers beneath the curtain. He was here! The magnitude of that, of his day in/day out devotion to me, is immeasurable.

Mark was a regular. He and the staff greeted each other like old friends. They joked around when the nurses came in to give me my medications — I was on quite a few of them — or when they helped me to use the bathroom or take a shower.

It took a few weeks, but eventually I could watch television without feeling too upset over the fact that the CNN anchor could talk and walk, or the local weatherman seemed to hardly have a care in the world besides announcing the weekend weather forecast. Sometimes we watched a movie or Mark read to me.

Sleeping in rehab was always an adventure. At about eight o'clock every night, the nurse gave me Ativan to help me sleep, and every night it took at least an hour before I finally dropped off. And that doesn't mean I wasn't tired. I was so exhausted by eight that I could barely keep my eyes open. It was July, and still light until about nine thirty. Mark would close the blinds and keep the room lights low as soon as the nurse came in with my nightly dose, but no matter what, every time I closed my eyes and started to doze off into a glorious and much-needed sleep, vertigo kicked in—and mercilessly. The room whirled like a top even with my eyes closed. I literally had to grab the bed rail and hold on for the ride.

When I finally did fall asleep, my head would list ever so slightly to the left or right, kicking off the vicious spin of dizziness again, and I would jolt awake, popping up in bed like it was some sort of springboard. I'd yell, "Dizzy!" and then lie down again, very slowly and carefully, and begin to doze off. In my first days at rehab, Mark would jump up and rush to my bedside to calm me down every time that dizzy/wake-up happened. But as the weeks went by, we both knew it was a nightly experience and it had to play out that way. Eventually, Mark simply needed to shout "You're okay!" from his pullout bed and I'd be calmed down. Until the next episode of dizziness. This routine repeated itself twenty or thirty times a night, until the Ativan finally kicked in and knocked me out. At two or three a.m. I'd wake, relieved to know that most of the night had passed and morning was on its way. I had survived another hellish night.

An endless stream of visitors passed in and out of my room at rehab. I loved visitors. Seeing the faces of family and friends night after night helped me remember who I was, that I was still the old Valerie, that I still mattered. I had visited people in the hospital before, but I understood now what a difference visitors make. They showed me I mattered, and they brought a little normalcy back into my life. I could live vicariously through their tales of the everyday and feel like I belonged.

The first time a visitor came to see me, I could sense their initial hesitation, even fear; they had no idea what they were about to see. I would hear their footsteps come to a stop right outside my door. Cautiously, they would peek into my room and then they'd come inside and greet me in my bed. Sometimes they had tears in their eyes. Sometimes they just looked frightened. Sometime later my friend and hairstylist, Dana, told me he was hesitant when he first visited me because he didn't know what to expect or how bad my condition was. People couldn't help but equate stroke with severe disability. And I was afraid, too, afraid my visitors expected a twisted, drooling-from-one-side-of-the-mouth grossly disfigured and incoherent person. I was bad off, but I wasn't that. I made sure to greet my visitors as I normally as I could and put everyone at ease as much as possible.

One night, I had an extremely unusual visitor, a man by the name of Carlos Arredondo. My good friend Kim had contacted Carlos, the longtime peace activist who became well-known as a hero because of his role in rushing to the aid of the Boston Marathon bombing victims. Carlos, popularly known as "the man in the cowboy hat," was interested in my story, and arranged for a visit. Kim gave me ample notice that Carlos and his wife, Mel, would be coming to see me. Kim knew I couldn't handle surprises too well in this condition and knew I'd be horrified to be seen this way by a stranger, even though I had a good excuse for looking as I did.

My parents were visiting me when Carlos arrived. I was ecstatic when I caught the first glimpse of his trademark cowboy hat in my doorway. Since the terrorist attack at the Boston Marathon in April I had read so much about him, and I'd seen him countless times on TV.

Carlos and Mel greeted me warmly, then pulled up their chairs so I could see them easily from my bed. I didn't want to speak much if I could help it, and I was glad when Carlos took the reins. To my amazement he told me I inspired him with my courage in this ordeal.

"I've cheated death multiple times," he said, "and I've lived through the deaths of both of my sons." I knew that one of his sons was killed in Iraq in 2004 and it was reported that the other took his life on the last day of that war out of grief. Carlos said he had found a new purpose in life. He had become a suicide prevention activist, traveling the world to spread his message of hope. And now he was known internationally for rushing to the aid of Boston Marathon spectator Jeff Bauman, as he lay legless and bleeding to death on the sidelines. He had helped save Jeff's life.

Two inspirational people.

While nurses came and went, the group of us spent the evening in my room talking about overcoming hardships. I was deeply inspired by Carlos's personal strength and courage in the face of all the adversity he had endured. It was a profound experience, and exactly what I needed.

A few musician friends visited while I was in Spaulding Rehab. Grant is a friend I made through the Grammy organization, a bluegrass artist. He had come all the way from Rhode Island, a trip of almost two hours, to visit me, and it was the first time we'd met in person. Another friend, Lydia, a fellow jazz vocalist I've known since my days with Al Vega, visited. They appeared tentative when they first greeted me, but I think it was the loss of my singing voice that really haunted them. Losing your musical ability is a musician's worst nightmare.

My friend Steven, a Boston-area pianist, was touched by my story. We didn't know each other well, but we had played together at gigs in the past. He frequently played at Spaulding Rehab, entertaining patients, and he was familiar with the physical devastation that a stroke causes.

Perhaps most distressing for Steven was to know that I had lost my ability to sing. He knew me as the bubbly girl with the powerful voice. When he heard about my stroke and that I had lost my voice, he wanted to bring the music to me and lift my spirits.

The first time Steven saw me tears welled up in his eyes. He stood at the foot of the bed, where I could see him best, and spoke in a gentle, sincere voice. "I've come to play the piano for you. I don't care how your voice sounds. I want you to sing." Steven thought that bringing a sense of my former life to rehab would help to bring me back.

A nurse came in and helped me transfer to my chair, and Steven wheeled me into the recreation room, which contained an upright piano. Just seeing that piano put a spark of fire in me, a much-needed spark. I was still a singer, no matter how wretched my voice sounded.

That day was pivotal, the real start of an incredible journey back to a life of music. We sat at the piano side by side, me in my wheelchair and Steven on the piano bench. "What do you want to sing?" he asked, turning to me.

I fought back tears. "How about 'Stardust' by Artie Shaw?"

"Stardust" was one of my favorite songs. I had recorded it on my first CD with the Al Vega Trio. It was a difficult song to sing, but I was determined to do it.

Steven played "Stardust" on the piano and I began to sing. It sounded terrible!

Screechy! I could only scream the lyrics, but at least I mostly matched the pitch. Steven wiped tears from his eyes as we continued the song and I started to cry, too. I cried so much I could barely get through the song. But we did it.

Seeing Steven and having him treat me like a singer, like someone he was practicing songs with, made me feel like myself again. And his generosity in taking the time to visit me and play with me told me a lot about him as a person. A renewed sense of purpose filled me after that day in the recreation room. He promised me he'd come back soon, we'd do this again. I couldn't wait.

Later that same week, during my speech therapy session in Carla's office, through her window I saw something that at first glance appeared to be ordinary but was truly inspirational—a playground that had recently been named for Boston's one-time mayor, Tom Menino. A dedication ceremony was being held for Menino, who was dying of cancer.

I watched as a small group of well-dressed people gathered in the playground. "What's going on out there?" I asked Carla.

"They're having a dedication in honor of Mayor Menino," Carla replied.

And there he was, Tom Menino, the beloved former mayor of Boston, the man who led the city for more than two decades, enjoying the sunshine in the face of his terminal illness and cutting the ceremonial red ribbon. He walked around the playground talking to passersby and shaking hands with people who came up to greet him. He was having his moment in the sun. His determination to live normally was an inspiration, the latest inspiration of many I experienced on this journey. Mayor Menino died in October, less than three months later.

Hope is a strange thing. It can lift you up from your darkest hour or fool you into thinking that everything will be fine. Either way, without hope, I had nothing. I imagined myself onstage again, singing and dancing, and slowly, ever so slowly, began to believe it was possible.

Chapter Twelve

I T WAS THIRTY DAYS AFTER the stroke.

Physically, I was still fully slanted to the right. My tongue veered sharply to my right, my writing sloped off the upper right side of the page, even my belly button slanted. My face was numb and somehow tingly at the same time, and now my *right* eye drooped a bit, making it look like I was squinting. The damage to my brain stem had caused a related neurological condition called Horner syndrome, which resulted in a smaller pupil and a slightly closed eyelid in my right eye.

I had regained very little movement in my left arm and hand. My speech was okay, but my voice was high-pitched and still sounded like I had marbles in my mouth. No one knew why, but as an experienced singer I believed my vocal cord on the left side was likely damaged. I couldn't even feel it. It was a very rough sound and often I was unable to match pitch, with no style, tone, or timbre possible when I tried to sing.

Why won't my hand just move already? I begged to know. I willed and willed it, trying with all my might. It didn't move. *Listen, fingers. You guys are pieces of shit. Just friggin' move.* I cursed myself like a sailor. My left arm felt heavier than my car. I just wanted to move my fingers. Frustrated, I wondered how I could ever be allowed to go home in this condition.

Why did this happen to me? I asked the Universe yet again, sulking in my wheelchair. It was so easy to revert to despair, the negative thoughts always ready to take over my mind. It helped to think about the Boston Marathon bombing survivors at this very hospital, likely doing the same therapies that I was. They had been struck randomly. They had survived. They were thriving, or would be. They had walked through hell and come out on the other side.

An elderly man was staying in the room next door. He was about eighty years old I guessed, and he could walk and talk, no problem. He used both hands. Had he survived a stroke? Was he one of the lucky ones? I envied him. Eventually, I noticed a nurse always accompanied him when he walked about the unit. I overheard him once, and realized he had a form of dementia. He didn't make sense. Once, he wandered into my room believing it was his and proceeded to open my refrigerator and help himself to my stash of applesauce. I felt so foolish and shallow for thinking he was somehow luckier than me.

Every stroke patient suffers in his or her own way. The brain is a very complex organ and the damage a stroke inflicts on it, and on the mind and body as a result, is impossible to predict. After a stroke people may not be able to speak, yet they could have full use of their limbs. Others have cognitive problems. I was lucky to be alive and fully coherent and able to communicate. I also knew that the human brain has amazing resilience, or specifically, neuroplasticity. After a stroke, the brain has the capacity to create new neural pathways to accomplish what it did before the stroke. I was depending on that.

Before the stroke believed I only used a tiny percentage of my brain, which left me a lot to work with. I don't know if that line of reasoning is valid. But, undoubtedly, thinking I had extra space in my brain made recovery more possible.

My friend Lisa came to see me in rehab one day. "I have something for you," she said, handing me an envelope. Inside was a gift card for downloading songs off the Internet onto my iPad. I wanted to throw my arms around her.

I used that gift card to buy some Mozart pieces. Maybe listening to classical music would activate the neural pathways that move my left arm, fingers and leg, I hoped. I was sure I only used a small percentage of my brain—I'd heard we all do—so there had to be plenty of cells just waiting in the wings for something to do.

I had no idea how long it was going to take, but I was going to get there.

I love fun. Who doesn't, right? But how fun does it sound to be in the situation I was in? Not very. Fortunately for me, at rehab there was also recreational therapy, whose goal was to return me to experiencing the "fun" in life.

My guide on that journey was Leah, an energetic and enthusiastic recreational therapist, who started by taking me to the rehab playground one afternoon to play a game of bocce ball. I loved bocce. My father built a regulation-sized bocce court in our yard when I was a kid and I'd loved to play with anyone who was willing.

It was a hot summer day, so hot I needed to bring three small water bottles for a half-hour bocce game. Leah wheeled me to a grassy area in front of Spaulding, parked my chair, and helped me stand. She placed the ball in my left hand. That ball is heavy for anyone, but for me that day, it weighed a hundred pounds. Instantly, my hand curled into a fist from the muscle tone that was kicking in, in response to the ball. My hand was wet with sweat.

Increased tone is the archenemy of stroke patients. Efforts to regain muscle tone can result in an atrophied look and the inability to move. Sometimes, it creates an extreme tightness in the extremities that can be very painful. I didn't know which was worse — having a hand with muscle tone and grip, or having a lifeless hunk of flesh and bone. I opted for the muscle tone and grip.

"Let's go," I told Leah, like she could do anything to make this work! It just helped to say it out loud.

I tried to throw the ball and nothing happened — it stayed in my grasp. But at least I could grasp it, and I got to feel the grass under my feet. For that I was grateful. For our next excursion into "fun," Leah's intern, L.T., surprised me one afternoon with something different. "Guess what? I have a surprise for you," she said. Her eyes sparkled with her good secret.

"You're coming with me," L.T. said, pushing my wheelchair out of my room, where I'd been sitting for ten minutes, ready for my afternoon outing with her. We both laughed. Like I had a choice!

L.T. wheeled me down the hall and into her office area, where a large TV and microphone stands were set up. I was puzzled. She wheeled me in front of the TV and parked. Leah had joined us, and she pressed a button on a machine attached to the television. I watched in amazement as the lyrics to "Creep" by Radiohead flashed across the screen. It was the karaoke version of one of my favorite songs.

"Oooh!" I exclaimed. "I used to sing this song in one of my bands!" I was ready to kick some musical ass.

"Let's go!" said Leah, with a big smile.

She and L.T. helped me stand, then held me steady as Leah put a microphone in my left hand. My *left* hand. Really? The microphone kept slipping out of my grip. I didn't care. Leah put the mic back in my hand every time it slipped out.

I sang for three minutes. The entire song. My pitch was off. My voice cracked on every high note. The littlest movement I made sent the room in a spin. And I didn't care. My old life was back. I was standing and singing, and nothing could take that away.

I did karaoke again one afternoon with patients from the other floors. Some had spinal cord injuries. Others were recovering from amputations or suffered a different type of brain injury. Leah thought this would be a great opportunity to socialize with fellow patients while doing something I loved — singing!

Life was so much worse for many other patients at Spaulding Rehab. I was wheeled into a recreation room, where I was met with a roomful of patients in wheelchairs, some with seizure-protection helmets on their heads or with tubes coming out of their noses, some with both. Some had missing limbs. Right away, I realized how lucky I was, how much worse things could have been for me, and I was filled with gratitude.

We all took turns singing. First, I sang Whitney Houston's "I'm Every Woman." It sounded horrible, but I yelled my way vivaciously through the song, not caring that I was off-key. What choice did I have? I mangled the tune, but I was singing.

Just holding the microphone was breathing new life into my now mostly listless soul. I missed performing for an audience so dearly.

I had to keep going. I had to try.

⚜

In early July, Alex had a question for me. "What do you think about going to the café down the street and getting a coffee with me? It'll be good to get out in public again."

Go out in public? Like this? Would I have the stamina for the Boston summer heat for more than five minutes? Would I be gawked at by the other café patrons? I hadn't interacted with anyone but medical staff and friends and family for over a month. I shared my concerns with Alex, who gave me the best answer possible. "Girl, you're a performer, right? You love attention."

She was right! People could gawk at me all day long and I'd eat it up. "Let's go!" I said. Alex and I planned on buying a cookie and a drink at the café. It sounded absolutely fantastic.

The next Monday, Alex asked me if I remembered what we had arranged to do today. I hesitated for a moment. What was the name of the café? I knew it was in Charlestown, where we were now, but I didn't get into Charlestown that much, other than for my occasional courthouse appearances. I was a tad preoccupied with other things at the moment — it had been a bad night of sleep, as usual, and this was my first activity of the day.

"Remember?" said Alex. "We're going to get something *round...*" She motioned like we were playing a game of charades, drawing the shape of a circle.

I liked Alex and appreciated everything she did for me, but I had to hold back my laughter on this one lest she'd think I was laughing at her. *Gee, I don't know, how about a friggin' cookie?* I wanted to tell her I had a stroke, not a lobotomy! I had to learn to be careful to avoid blunders like this in the future, despite their momentary comedic relief. In my condition, any innocuous forgetfulness or slip of the tongue could land me an extended stay in rehab, or give me a notation of possible dementia on my medical chart.

"We're going to a café near here," I told her. "We're walking there to have a drink and a cookie."

I wore my leg brace and used my cane for the walk to the café. Leah and her intern, L.T., came along, each of them taking turns pushing my wheelchair down portions of the sidewalk, the boardwalk, a small pedestrian footbridge, and some graveled terrain. There was a lot going on out there, something you don't notice unless you're riding along in a chair or plodding along so slowly you could probably knit the sleeve of a sweater while you walked. At times, we stopped so I could I get into the chair to have a short rest.

It was over ninety degrees that day, and the humidity was off the charts. The sun beat down, and at times I felt like I might pass out. But I was determined not to. I moved cautiously, watching every step to make sure it worked. "I hope you're okay with getting there by Christmas," I joked.

Everyone laughed. I knew they wanted the best for me, they wanted to see this work.

By the time we got to the café I was thoroughly exhausted. I could barely walk. I limped toward the entrance, leaning heavily into my cane. Just then, I noticed a man getting out of his van. He was just an ordinary person patronizing a café on a hot summer day. I don't know what made me look at him, but seeing him, something resonated deep inside me. He was a symbol of what I once was.

"Look at him," I remarked somberly. "I was like him until a few weeks ago." My eyes welled up with tears.

Everyone seemed surprised I'd be upset to arrive at the café. One of them suggested I focus on what a lovely warm summer day it was in Boston.

A lovely warm summer day in Boston? I didn't know whether to laugh or cry. Did she honestly think I would be happy to think about that? She didn't know what having a stroke truly felt like, what spending the summer — and maybe longer — in rehab was like.

Not a second passed without my thinking of the stroke and what it had done to my life. I was supposed to be in Rome. Rome!

One of the most beautiful places on earth. Yet I was learning to walk again. I was supposed to be singing jazz under the stars in Perugia eating spoonfuls of Nutella gelato. And here I was stuck limping through the streets of Charlestown hoping to score a cookie and maybe catch a view of the Mystic River. Thinking of the sunshine over Charlestown and walking past a trash dumpster wasn't going to somehow make me elated.

A stroke is the quickest and slickest pickpocket on earth. Without any warning or chance of protecting yourself, your life disappears in the time it takes to blink an eye. But a stroke also forces you to learn to cope. It forces you to have patience. It gives you a new perspective on life. You can understand how a disabled person feels because you are one. You can relate to the hardships of illness because you live with them every second. You know what it's like to be reduced to nothing and rise out of the ashes to reinvent your life. And you find out what you're made of as you pick yourself up from despair again and again and remember your life *can* be reinvented.

Chapter Thirteen

THE REHAB STAFF OFTEN SEEMED quite concerned about my having full command of my mental faculties. They were on the lookout for even the slightest deviation in my behavior from their idea of "normal." I couldn't blame them. After all, I had suffered a good-sized stroke in my brain stem. My neck arteries had torn. My doctors classified the tear as spontaneous. Because of the extreme accompanying stiff neck and pain, I believe the tear likely started with the neck turn in bed.

Mental deficits are a common side effect of stroke. But I had none. Sure, I was a little anxious. But considering I'd had a stroke that had nearly killed me, any nervousness or anxiety on my part was justified. I gave myself a free pass in the "freaking out" department and didn't care what anyone thought. No one was living my life, I didn't know those people in the outside world, and I was determined do to what I had to do to recover. I also knew I had to put my education and mental acuity to work if I ever wanted to go home. So I stayed focused. *Really* focused. I reminded myself I had survived law school and the bar exam. I could do whatever the Spaulding Rehab staff asked of me.

One day, the staff psychologist, a very kind and serious inquisitive older man, visited me. He closed the door to my room, in case I needed to make a confession, I supposed, then sat down and asked me a bunch of questions about what was going on in my life at the time of the stroke. I knew he was searching for clues as to why this had happened to me. "Did you use drugs?" he asked. "You can tell me. This is totally confidential between us." I told him no, I didn't use drugs. "Were you particularly stressed out?" I wasn't.

I told the psychologist that on the night of my stroke my husband thought I was having a panic attack or a bad dream because I had wakened suddenly from a deep sleep unable to move or see straight, and my arm was clenched to my chest uncontrollably.

That would scare the pants off anyone.

Somehow, from my responses to his questions and the fact that my husband initially thought the stroke was just a bad dream, the psychologist hinted that I also may have had a sleep issue. I know I have a type A personality; I've had it since birth. But a sleep issue? I usually have great dreams and before the stroke I never had sleep problems. I was already fighting this war on so many fronts, the last thing I needed was another diagnosis added to the mix. Some things just don't have a definitive answer, and the cause of the arteries tearing in my neck that night is one of them. I suspected the cause to be that fateful turn of my neck, but I will never know for certain.

The psychologist visited me in my room every day for a while, checking to see if I needed someone to talk to, or whether I'd had any more bad dreams. We discussed all sorts of things, and he expressed a sincere interest in my feelings about this ordeal. My opinion of him changed quite rapidly after that, especially when I learned he was also a pianist.

Next, a staff psychiatrist came to see me. In confidence, he asked if I'd ever used cocaine; using that drug could cause a stroke. Ah, the mysteries of the unknown were obviously not passing muster with this group. They had to blame the stroke on something. I can't say I didn't understand that. I wanted to blame it on something, too.

But from everything I'd been told by some of the best neurologists, the tear just happened.

I wasn't on drugs. I didn't smoke anything, ever. I ate well and I was always very slim. I was the picture of health, young and energetic. Until the night I went to bed with a neck ache and woke up two hours later having a stroke.

That was it.

Last, the staff neuropsychologist came to see me. I'll call him Dr. Montague (he reminded me of the Harvey Korman character in *High Anxiety*). When Dr. Montague waltzed into my room, my first thought was that he was an affable young man.

"Well, this is kind of a crappy situation, isn't it?" he said, in a tone I knew all too well from my career as an attorney. I knew what he was doing. He was trying to elicit a reaction from me. I figured he thought that's what he needed to do initially to assess my mental state. Though I knew all this, I started to get teary-eyed again. *No shit, Sherlock, I thought.* Was this guy serious? Still, despite my annoyance, I found the man oddly amusing.

Dr. Montague proceeded to perform a cognitive assessment exam on me, which consisted of my drawing stick figures and a weird looking clock, repeating words and numbers, and counting backwards in increments of four or six, and basically anything else you can think of that you might have done in preschool. He explained that he was testing for executive function and whether or not the stroke had affected me mentally. He then told me he had heard from the staff that I was slightly off.

Now, that was *not* the smartest thing to say to me, unless his purpose was to get a rise out of me. I was on fire now. I had one side that was operational, but I wanted to kick the ass of whoever had told him that. And the term "executive function"? That really irked me. I cringed every time he used those words during the session. I hadn't lost any executive function. I could have run his entire medical practice from my bed! Sure, I was a little drugged up from the Ativan they'd given me to fight the dizziness and calm any anxiety, but it wasn't like I was frothing at the mouth or hallucinating that I was Napoleon. This doctor had no clue who he was dealing with. I wanted him to take a shot at me, to hit me with his most difficult exam. Then he'd see who I really was.

I felt like I was on trial sitting with Dr. Montague in my rehab room, my wheelchair pulled up to the tray table, which doubled as my "desk" for the moment. Dr. Montague then gave me instructions and timed my responses. "You have one minute to copy this drawing of a clock. Go."

I drew the freaking clock and had enough time to shoot him a look that screamed "If I wasn't in this wheelchair, I'd kick your ass into the middle of next week."

"Now, tell me all the animals that begin with the letter A."

Uh oh. Here we go again, I thought. Speech Therapy 2.0. Geez, I knew this test was not going to help my case. I knew I should have been more interested in animals when I was growing up, maybe had a pet turtle or something. Then at least I'd be able to name an animal beginning with the letter T. In high school biology, my friend Carolann and I were too busy playing with the skeleton the teacher kept in the back of the classroom or doodling the lyrics to Duran Duran songs on my Trapper Keeper.

Dr. Montague said he had been told the staff members were concerned about me, as I appeared to be a very chatty patient. This exam was beginning to go over like a fart in church. A "chatty patient"?

"Apparently, you tell your tales of woe to everyone that comes to treat you," he said, "doctors, nurses, assistants."

I had to admit he was right, I did talk to everyone I could talk to. But no one seemed to mind. And I knew exactly what I was doing. I was afraid that if I were quiet, I would lose my voice like in those crazy dreams where you open your mouth to scream and nothing comes out. The art of talking was a reassurance factor for me. I was sorry if I drove the staff crazy with my endless babbling, but babbling only signified one thing to me: It meant I still had a voice. And there was more. I wanted the staff to know I had a working brain. I wasn't "chatty" because of a decrease in my brain function. But I didn't tell the doctor this. If I told him, it would look to him like I was trying to rationalize my behavior. And yet another reason I was "chatty" was because I had to get my mind off the constant dizziness or it would consume me. Talking was calming, even if just for a few moments.

I considered what he'd said to me: *Apparently, you tell your tales of woe to everyone that comes to treat you.* What else was there to talk with them about? Was I supposed to ask about their day? Their home lives? I told them what had gotten me here, and that was about it, that's what I had. I didn't care about anyone's opinion of me. I was never going to see them after rehab. If they thought I was a whack job, it was fine with me.

Dr. Montague would never understand, so I didn't even try to explain. There were even more good reasons for my being "chatty." If I stayed quiet, the sheer intensity of the fear of another stroke, compounded by the issues presented by my partial paralysis, was unbearable. I had devised this coping plan early in my hospital stay. Plus, I'm a talker. I didn't become a lawyer and a performer by being quiet.

We finished the tests and Dr. Montague put his papers in his briefcase, snapped it shut, and left my room, telling me he'd be back in a few days with the results. "Thanks for stopping by," I muttered, rolling my eyes as he walked out. His mental function test results were going in my circular file as soon as possible.

Chapter Fourteen

THE BLOOD CLOT IN MY brain stem had erased my entire vestibular system (the parts of the inner ear that help control balance, among other things) in a matter of seconds, which was why I experienced such unrelenting dizziness. That clot, I'd been told by rehab staff, would likely disappear in about six months from when it started. I was given daily doses of blood thinners to keep my blood from clotting while my arteries healed, followed by an aspirin every day for the rest of my life.

The relentless dizziness was perhaps the biggest limitation I faced in rehab. If I could experience a brief respite from the spinning, I could blast through my physical therapy, working intensively instead of stopping every few minutes to focus. But I never had much respite, so I had to force myself to soldier on. I knew that the first weeks after a stroke are vital to recovery. The connections within my brain needed to be reestablished, and time was passing quickly. I had to take action and not lie about waiting for the dizziness to end. I had to accept the dizziness and refuse to allow it to hinder my recovery.

My father had spent three years on a ship when he was in the Navy in the South Pacific during the 1950s. He had told me years before that on shore leave he'd walk with a slant because of all that time at sea. That's how I felt. It was like relearning to walk on a dinghy in the middle of a typhoon.

It was a major feat to relearn to walk while dizzy and unable to turn my head.

Writing, too, was hard when I was so dizzy; my handwriting veered off to one corner of the page. I got dressed while dizzy and I ate while dizzy. In fact, there was nothing I did while in rehab without being dizzy. I kept my head as still as possible, staring straight ahead, with the hope the dizziness wouldn't be so violent. But it was always there.

I thought of my blind friend, Noe. He relies on his other senses, including touch, and he lives an amazing life. He is a renowned guitarist and his blindness doesn't limit or define him. I wanted to be like that too. I tried his method, and found it worked for me, it was the way to go. Using my other senses, I succeeded in relearning even the most basic of activities while staring straight ahead and focusing on a single object. I felt for everything outside my field of vision and within my reach using my imagination and my inner compass as a guide. I found railings in the hallways and paper towels in the bathroom, the nurse call button on my bed, the food on my plate. Relying on my sense of touch was working like a charm.

By mid-July, my left hand was still barely moving. Every day I mentally moved all of my fingers with the hope that my thoughts would soon control my movements. But nothing changed. I repeatedly made a fist with my right hand and quickly opened it as wide as I could, hoping it would spark a connection between left and right. Eventually, the pinky finger on my left hand started to come alive. Granted, it was a tiny movement, but it was something. That millimeter of success propelled me toward my goal of more. With the help of my working right arm, I started moving my left arm from side to side just a few inches. It was passive movement, but I wanted my body to remember how it felt to move.

Soon, I could do more things, everyday things we take for granted, like wash my hands and reach for a hand towel. I placed my left hand in the bathroom sink and rubbed liquid soap all over it. I didn't have the strength to move my left arm under water, so mostly I put the soap on my left hand and lathered it with my right before placing my left arm under the faucet with my right hand. Also with my right hand, I felt for the paper towel rack on the wall by the sink and tore one from the holder. I was learning to function with one only fully working side.

One night, after my evening visitors had left, Mark started to change his clothes for another long night on the pullout couch.

"Can we get someone in here to wheel me into the bathroom?" I said. "I just drank a whole bottle of water and I have to pee like a racehorse."

"Hit the buzzer," said Mark, nodding over his shoulder toward the bed, where he knew I had the handheld nurse's buzzer at the ready. I rang the buzzer for the nurse, but everyone was busy tending to other patients on my floor, I was told. I must have waited ten minutes, but those ten minutes felt like hours. It was torture. I could barely hold on any longer when two nurses casually entered my room with a set of fresh sheets in hand. "Oh," one of them said, nonchalantly. "You don't need new sheets? Didn't you wet the bed?"

"No!" I triumphantly exclaimed. "I'm still waiting to go to the bathroom." They seemed shocked. I assumed they were expecting I peed the bed and they were there to change my bed linens. The fact that I was able to hold my pee for an extended period of time meant that I was turning another corner.

After that day, for the first time in too long, I was allowed to use the bathroom by myself for some brief, cherished moments of privacy. I didn't have to be in the presence of one or two nurses, who would wipe my ass. I was able to wipe my own ass, and it felt great. I still had to be escorted to the bathroom and hoisted in and out of my wheelchair, but at least I could pee on the toilet in peace.

The next week, during one of my occupational therapy sessions, my left thumb started to move ever so slightly. Granted, it wasn't much, but it moved! I had pinky movement *and* a thumb. Two fingers! This was big.

And there was progress in another part of my body: My left leg was noticeably stronger. That meant I could sit in bed and cross and uncross my legs, and I did that, constantly. Back and forth. Right over left, left over right. I fancied myself a contortionist of sorts. I believed the secret to recovering my body was repetitive movement. I didn't care how I was perceived. I moved every second I could. I had to make those connections in my brain. Retraining my body became the highlight of my day.

Finally, in the second week of July, my medical team made a huge and thrilling decision: it was time for me to go home. Home! No nursing home for me! Dr. Lee, the staff doctor for the stroke patients, visited later that glorious day and told me I was going to use their outpatient rehab center to continue my therapy while living at home.

I had to make so many calls to make! My bathroom had to be fitted with bars and a shower chair. I needed a stool to get into my bed. The pool guys had to install a railing for me so I could walk into my pool to exercise my legs and arms and strengthen them.

The excitement was overwhelming, and I was also a little scared. What if I fell?

What if the dizziness never went away? No one knew the answers to these things. Dr. Lee said, "We hope the dizziness will resolve, but stroke recovery is impossible to predict. Each stroke is different." His lack of complete certainty, although understandable, frightened me. Stay like this for the rest of my life, unable to do anything except go to the bathroom or walk on a slant to the kitchen to get something to eat? I couldn't bear to live like that.

Saying good-bye to my nurses was very emotional. These people had treated me like more than just a patient. I would miss Vivian, my evening nurse, the one who had comforted me through the dizziness every night. She was soft-spoken and gentle, invariably the one by my bedside during all those horrible nights when I was so dizzy I'd have to hold onto the bed rail, crying in agony and begging the spinning to stop. Vivian told me to have faith, that it was only a matter of time before I would be so strong on my left side I'd be able to throw a decent punch. She assured me I'd look back on this as a distant memory one day. Michi was my morning nurse, the one who gave me my pills and took my vital signs. She would ask my opinion about legal topics, which made me feel like a lawyer and not just a stroke survivor. Kameesha dressed and bathed me almost every day, carefully drying each of my toes with a towel every time she showered me. I loved that. I had never cared so much about my own toes in my life. I felt like she was giving me a salon pedicure every time I took a shower.

I said good-bye to my therapists, and thanked them for everything they'd done for me. If it hadn't been for the excellent care I'd received at Spaulding Rehab, I surely wouldn't be at the level of recovery I was. I would miss them very much.

On the day I was scheduled to go home, "what-ifs" swirled in my head as I waited for my parents and Mark to come and get me. I was leaving my safe zone, Spaulding Rehab, and venturing into the real world. What if I needed an emergency medication?

What if my blood pressure went up? What if I had stroke symptoms again?

When they arrived, my mother packed my belongings into a couple of boxes. My father asked about a handicapped placard for my car. "We should get the placard now. You don't want Mark to have to park a mile away from the door if you go to CVS or something."

Ahh, CVS. To walk into a store to buy something as everyday as a greeting card or a bottle of nail polish. I couldn't wait to do those things again. We decided my father would take care of getting the handicapped placard for me, which left me in the clear, since Dr. Lee had to sign the application for it and my father and I had both asked the doctor for the signed application more than once. I didn't want to take the chance of being labeled a pain in the ass. I couldn't risk Dr. Lee thinking I was perseverating and report it as a concern to the neuropsychologist, my not-so-dear Dr. Montague.

After a few hours, we had the signed application for the handicapped placard and we were ready to go. An orderly escorted me to the ground level front door.

Mark would be picking me up in my car and was bringing it around to the front entrance. My heart pounded as I passed the elevators on the stroke unit for the last time, and I waved to everyone I saw — nurses, doctors, even other patients and their visiting families. I was grinning from ear to ear. I was going home. I was still dizzy and hardly had a left side, but I couldn't have been happier.

Downstairs, the orderly transferred me to one of the temporary public wheelchairs available in the lobby and whisked away the wheelchair I had used throughout my stay in rehab. This new one looked like a golf cart, or one of those oversized faux wheelchairs you sometimes see in airports. It was awkward and I hoped I wouldn't fall out of it. Then he left.

Sitting in that chair holding my cane, I was alone for the first time in over a month. I watched visitors scurry in and out of the lobby. I was sweaty and nervous, but I felt free. I was no longer a patient!

Mark pulled up and I saw my car for the first time since the stroke, my white Mercury Milan. Mark had taken good care of it. I was leaving in style.

But what was next? How was I going to manage getting out of this cart and into the passenger seat? Mark held me up while I transferred to the seat, wearing my leg brace and using my cane. I didn't know how long I could stay standing. I barely escaped knocking my head against the doorframe. But I did it.

As we pulled away from Spaulding Rehab Hospital, the scenery looked surreal. I knew the area well, but the buildings looked as if someone had repainted them in brighter hues that morning. The sun shone through the car windows, making me squint in order to see. I felt like I hadn't seen daylight in years.

Mark merged into the stream of rush-hour traffic, as tense as I was. It seemed like we were going so fast! I hadn't been in a vehicle other than an ambulance since the stroke, and every turn threw me into an even bigger whirl of dizziness. "Don't go so fast!" I pleaded (over and over again). Mark promised he wasn't driving more than thirty miles an hour. On the highway. In the slow lane. He tried to avoid every bump in the road.

The other cars frightened me flying by so fast, darting in front of us, coming up next to us one after the other like we all were on an airport landing strip. It hurt my brain to see them whiz by the passenger window. Could I ever get behind the steering wheel again myself one day and navigate situations I had never realized were so complicated?

And so incredibly fast! I reminded myself that for twenty-five years I had practically lived in my car, navigating the narrowest of Boston streets with one hand on the steering wheel, a hot chocolate in the other. The hardest of driving conditions was as easy as walking across my living room. Would I be a passenger for the rest of my life?

No way.

Chapter Fifteen

A T LAST, WE MADE THE turn onto our street. Everything looked like I'd seen it yesterday. It was as if time had stopped the night I was taken away by ambulance. *Didn't I just get that new bathing suit I bought from a catalog delivered?* I remembered running to my neighbor's house to pick it up the day before the stroke.

The houses on our street looked nice with their flower gardens and neatly manicured front lawns.

Mark pulled into our driveway and as he did, a colorful banner came into view. Taped to the wood siding just under living room window, in big multicolored letters, the sign read "Welcome Home." Kim's two daughters had made it for me as a homecoming gift, I would learn, two special girls as loving and kind as their mother. It brought tears to my eyes to know that my friends and their children cared about me so much they would do this for me.

My in-laws and parents waited at the front door while Mark helped me climb slowly out of the car. I manually placed my left leg outside of the car and Mark handed me my cane, steadying me with his hands while I stood as still as possible. Every motion increased my dizziness. I felt huge compassion for my grandmother, who I'd been impatient with as a teenager when I had to wait for her to get in and out of the car.

I'm sure she didn't like moving at a snail's pace, and physically, she was probably in pain.

The humidity made the air dense and heavy. It felt like a weight on my shoulders and on every limb. My family had put a chair in the walkway in case I needed it, and when Mark heard me say, "It's too much," panting after just a few steps, he brought it closer. I'd walked maybe five feet and had to sit down.

When I finally completed the journey from car to house and walked through the doorway, the smell of home gave me a fluttery thrill. It is an indescribable smell, something like pure joy after smelling hospital sanitizer 24/7 for too long. My family stood by while I took it all in, glancing around the room to see my belongings—my books were still in my bookcase, my television was in the same spot. I went into the kitchen, which looked marvelously the same too, and slowly opened a cupboard to see if I could do it. Even that made me too dizzy, as I had to look up to see the contents of a shelf.

I went into the well-lit great room, happy for all its many windows that overlooked the yard and the street, and planted myself on my couch. This seemed a superb command center for my recovery, and I decided that was where I would sit all day, every day. Anything was better than lying in bed! And from this vantage point I could see the neighborhood kids playing in the street, I could watch any animals that wandered into my yard—a neighbor cat, maybe a scurrying squirrel—and if I turned slightly to the right I could see my precious swimming pool, blue and still as a pond on a completely calm day. My brain was in a fog and the room spun every few seconds, but I was so happy.

Right away, my mother set up a tray table next to the couch for my food and drinks, the TV remote control, and my iPad. I persuaded my parents to buy me a blood pressure monitor and oximeter to measure my heart rate so I could monitor myself constantly and be sure I wasn't having another stroke.

I sat on the couch all day.

At about six that night, there was a news report of a tornado warning in my county and we had to get down to the basement as quickly as we could. Was this the Universe's idea of a sick joke? A tornado warning on my first day home from rehab? I couldn't even walk, let alone run to the basement. And there was no way I could do it quickly, either. I was more scared of falling than I was of the tornado itself.

"I can't believe this," I muttered.

"You don't need to go downstairs, you know. It's just a bunch of thunderstorms. It will pass. But if you really want to, I'll help you," Mark said.

"Okay. Let's go," I replied.

I was wearing my leg brace, and every step would be a huge production. I picked up my cane and let Mark practically carry me to the stairwell, where I took hold of the wrought iron railing with my right hand. Mustering every bit of strength I could and powering over my fear of the staircase (the few stairs in our home seemed so steep!), I walked five steps. Five steps and I could be at the landing. I made a game out of it, counting the steps down until I got to my destination. The counting out loud kept me calm.

Mark wasn't bothered by the possibility of a tornado. Weather events never bothered him. He could swim in a monsoon without a care in the world. Me, on the other hand, I'm all about safety. I'm always the one who won't drive in a snowstorm, who stocks up on hurricane supplies if there's a squall as far away as Florida. I unplug every household appliance in a thunderstorm.

We stayed downstairs for an hour until the tornado advisory passed. I kept most of my musical equipment in the basement and I missed the many nights I stayed in this room for hours practicing songs or playing my violin. My old karaoke machines, PA system, and recording equipment were neatly arranged against the wall as I had left them over a month earlier. They were reminders of my old life. My eyes filled with tears as I thought about those days, but I didn't want Mark to see me cry. After all, Mark had spent the last month sleeping in a hospital room and comforting me through some pretty rough times. He deserved a break from sadness. I quickly wiped my eyes with my right hand and we made our way to the stairwell.

"Hold onto my arm," Mark said, helping me up the stairs from the basement to the main level of our home. I felt like I had just worked out for six hours but I had only managed to climb a total of ten steps. I was ready for bed.

That night, I was excited to sleep in my own bed for the first time in almost two months. But it quickly became apparent that I had a huge problem. I couldn't get into the bed! Mark had to carry me and try to plunk me down on the bed ever so carefully, so as to not move my neck or aggravate my dizziness. It was difficult and we needed an easier method. Mark suggested we call my father for help. My father spent the 1960s as an aircraft mechanic and flight instrument instructor for a large airline. If he could fix a 737, he would surely be able to devise a way to get me into bed.

Great, I thought. I'm calling my dad to help put me to bed. Although parents only lived five minutes away, my dad was pushing eighty. But I knew he could figure something out. He was resourceful that way.

Within the hour, after racing to the store to buy me a step stool, my dad was there to save the day. Mark helped me out of the wheelchair and I held onto him while stepping about one foot off the ground and onto the stool. Step by step, I gradually turned to face the bed, grasping the back of the stool with my good hand. I turned around slowly to face the bed and waited for Mark to plunk my body down.

Ah! Success! But I was still dizzy. At least now I could yell "dizzy" in my own bed. After an hour or so of dizzy/wake-up cycles, I fell asleep in my own bed for the first time in two months.

The next morning, I had to figure out how I was going to accomplish taking a shower at home. Our formerly chic-ly decorated bathroom turned into something out of an "I've fallen and I can't get up" commercials. I had a shower chair along with a handheld nozzle in my shower, along with a newly installed metal bar. My pink bathroom rugs were removed so I wouldn't trip over them.

My mother and Mark helped to me into the shower.

There is something definitely NOT sexy about your husband and your mother working together to give you a shower. I'm just thankful neither of them were naked as they worked together fully clothed in the production that was showering me. That image alone would have sent me straight to the mental ward. But I was too dizzy to think about anything other than getting myself clean.

I could brush my teeth, thankfully, by feeling for the toothpaste, as I couldn't see it unless it was directly in front of me. Brushing my hair was difficult, though I could do it; every touch of the brush to my head made me even dizzier, as if the brush was jiggling my brain. I wore no makeup most of the time. Putting on makeup was a gargantuan effort because I needed both hands to do it, and I had so little energy. I often resorted to smearing bright red lipstick, my trademark color, onto my lips. Those bright red, retro-style lips served as a tiny reminder that the old me was in there somewhere. I just had to try to overlook that my lips looked slightly uneven when I smiled.

This was my daily routine at home: I'd wake at five a.m., eat a small snack and sip the glass of water that Mark always left on a tray table we kept next to the bed. I waited for Mark to wake up and make me breakfast in bed. After a few weeks I was strong enough to limp to the kitchen by myself using my cane. I'd carry my bowl of cereal to my spot in the great room and set it on the tray there, then I'd sit and rest for however long it took to recover from all that.

I was hungry, but just the act of eating would be a new ordeal. The sound of chewing my cereal was so loud in my brain that it frequently gave me a panic attack. Was I having another stroke?

I was terrified of having another stroke. Every day I felt twinges of pain in my neck, and it scared the heck out of me. It was nothing, I was sure (in rational moments), probably an effect of not turning my neck for months combined with sensations of my arterial dissection healing. I still couldn't move my head to either side, but I was moving more in general than I had at rehab.

Inevitably, every morning I felt bizarre, like I'd been clonked in the head. I was in a brain fog. It was as if a cloud of haze enveloped my being. Getting dressed was surreal, and I couldn't do it alone. I would wait for my mother to come over and have both her and my husband help. My arms just didn't bend the way they used to, and I couldn't get them into the sleeves of my shirts. I had to settle for oversized T-shirts.

Still lying on the bed in my guest bedroom was a new dress I had bought to wear in Italy. I bought it a few days before the stroke. It was a sexy, skintight dress that required a good deal of dexterity in my arms to get on. I wanted to wear it, to feel it on my body, to feel *good* in my body! I hounded my husband to help me into it until he finally gave in. But I couldn't get the dress on. I dissolved in tears midway through and gave up. Sure, I was home, but my old life didn't quite fit me.

Each night we'd eat a dinner Mark cooked for us. Mark is an amazing cook, so we always ate healthy meals of chicken or fish with vegetables. Eating caused a burning sensation that no amount of water could relieve, but I knew I had to keep my strength up.

We took a walk in the early evenings, an attempt at creating a new kind of normal. Usually, I'd limp as far as the foot of the driveway and then sheer exhaustion would hit. I wanted to lie down right there and stop the spinning, but I'd take a deep breath and drink some water (I always had water handy) and then we'd make the journey back home. I'd rest after this; nausea set in every evening around seven. When Mark tucked me into bed like a child — he was afraid I'd fall off if the sheets weren't tight around me — I'd laugh sometimes. "You realize in our old life we'd be getting ready to go out about now," I might say.

Once in bed, I gulped down my evening pills, then I'd wait to recover from the immense effort it took to sit up and swallow. The dizziness was particularly heinous at night, so I would carefully position a mountain of pillows around my neck. Next, it was time for my nightly blood pressure check and stroke self-tests. I'd repeatedly puff out my cheeks to see if they were equal, stick out my tongue to make sure it wasn't veering to one side, and check the size of my pupils to be sure they were even. It was like I'd developed some sort of stroke-induced OCD.

After my little medical exam, I'd amuse myself for a while, maybe playing a few brain games on my iPad to keep my mind sharp. I had developed an obsessive habit of researching my symptoms on my iPad nightly and relaying my self-diagnoses to Mark, describing the life-threatening complications and illnesses I could potentially get. "I think I could get diabetes or high blood pressure because of the stroke. And what if I have weak arteries all over my body? I could get other neurological disorders!" I shouted from the bed.

Mark knew better than to give my worries much attention. His rationality helped me come back to earth.

My dreadful anxiety always peaked at night. I was terrified of sleeping. Who could blame me? After all, I'd torn my neck arteries in my sleep, and a few days later I'd had a stroke in my sleep. Needless to say, sleep and I weren't exactly best buddies.

I was scared out of my wits that I wouldn't wake up. I'd doze off, then almost immediately wake up, startled and yelling "Help!" Mark had to come running in from the room next door, worried something had happened to me. "What's the matter? I'm fine. I don't know what you're so nervous about," I often said as I became fully awake.

I did this repeatedly, several times each night, for months. I came to the conclusion that my husband was truly a saint, tolerating all this ridiculousness. Not to mention, I drank water by the gallons every day, so poor Mark had the unenviable task of wheeling me to the bathroom every hour or so and helping me onto the toilet when I was too tired to limp there on my own. It was humiliating, but anything was better than being in the hospital with two nurses wiping my ass. Yes, I was home again, and the great adventure of recovery was on.

Chapter Sixteen

A FTER COMING HOME FROM REHAB, one of the first things I did was make an appointment at the world-renowned Massachusetts General Hospital Voice Center. I had to know if the problem was that my vocal muscles on the left couldn't move, or was it something neurological and my brain had lost the ability to perform the physical act of singing. I knew something of their work from colleagues who had been treated at the Center, and I knew doctors there had worked with famous singers including Julie Andrews, Adele, and Steven Tyler. If musical legends could suffer through being unable to sing, I knew that I, a relatively small-time vocalist who cared more about singing than just about anything else, had to pull myself together and do it too.

It's the emotional devastation of losing your voice that anyone with such a loss suffers, whether you are an award-winning singer or someone who sings in the shower. For me, losing my voice meant losing my identity. I longed for that euphoria that singing gave me every time I held a note and heard the note progress, resonating and giving way to a sweet vibrato after a few seconds. A piece of my soul was missing. Seeing renowned musicians overcome vocal problems assured me that though I might never truly "get over" the loss of my singing voice, I could soldier on. I could get *somewhere*, anyway. I had to try.

On the day of my appointment at the MGH Voice Center, Mark wheeled me along the uneven sidewalks of downtown Boston to a discreet office building a few blocks from the main hospital. I entered the office suite, struck by how non-medical it was, with its mahogany accents and a windowed waiting room with an autographed photograph of Cher hanging on the wall next to photographs of other celebrity singers. A medical technician ushered me into the examination room, and I started to cry, afraid of what was undoubtedly coming next—the exam that would give me the answer I wanted more than anything and feared more than ever.

"If you want us to put your photo on the wall, too," the technician said, jovially, "you have to get scoped!" "Scoped" referred to a laryngoscopy, a common diagnostic test that singers are often given when seeking treatment for vocal cord or throat problems. The vocal folds are examined by inserting a metal instrument, the "scope," down the throat. The exam requires a topical anesthetic that numbs your throat for a few hours so that the doctor can perform the test. I'd always feared having to take a test like that someday, and here I was, asking for it. It scared the daylights out of me. The fact that I had only recently recovered my ability to swallow frightened me even more. I was terrified that if my throat were numbed it could stay that way and never come back. I agreed to the test, but only if I could do it without the anesthetic being sprayed in my throat. I am certain the medical technician thought I was insane.

A young doctor entered the room, and the exam began. "I was told you don't want an anesthetic. Are you *sure*? It'll wear off in just a few hours."

"I am sure," I replied. "I had a stroke and just got my ability to swallow back. I can't deal with losing it again. I'll do the test without it."

And with that, he began. Slowly, he began the procedure by inserting an instrument that looked something like a tuning fork down my throat. I gagged uncontrollably within moments. This was going to be a long day.

"I'm sorry," I told him, when he drew back. "Let's keep going. I'll try to control myself." But there was no way. My uncontrollable gagging continued.

"We need to stop," the doctor said. "You'll have to come back when you can have your throat numbed and we can do the test."

I was dejected and relieved—and I was also torn. My fear of the "scope" was immense, but I really needed to know what the problem was so I could get my voice back.

A kind female doctor came in to examine me. She asked me to sing a few notes and speak while she used her fingers to feel the sides of my neck. "I don't think your left vocal cord is paralyzed. I can feel both cords vibrating, although the left vocal cord feels quite weak. When you feel up to it we can give you a scope and make a diagnosis."

I almost fell off my chair. *Incredible news!* I likely had two working vocal cords. After the stroke, I was afraid I'd lost my left vocal cord forever. I couldn't swallow for days. In rehab I couldn't feel my left vocal cord vibrate whenever I placed my right thumb and index finger to my throat while howling a note. My speaking voice was hoarse and I spoke in a whiny whisper. This led me to believe my left cord was paralyzed but I will never know for certain because I was improving all the time. Maybe my singing voice was gradually waking up from its stroke-induced slumber.

I had to devote myself to getting stronger, not only through vocal exercises but also with the help of cardio training and the rehabilitation of my entire body. I was going to sing again.

I decided to compose an email to a few of my friends in Italy to let them know of my complete recovery and my return to singing. I didn't send the email, but writing to let people know I had returned cemented the idea that I was going to overcome this. I could hardly wait for the day I would press the "send" button on that email; it would signify that my darkest days were over.

Strokes create a sort of indescribable fatigue that is not correlated to physical exhaustion. It's mental exhaustion. My entire system was working on overdrive just to limp to the bathroom on a good day. A single visit from a friend drained me. I lost my breath just from having a conversation, and frequently had to cut visits short because of violent dizzy spells. After my visitor left I would spend the remainder of the day in bed, exhausted.

A few days after I my visit to the voice center at MGH, I scared myself. I was chewing my Rice Krispies at breakfast one morning with all of my senses on overdrive, as usual; just the act of chewing sounded like my jaw was connected to the sound system at Madison Square Garden. Suddenly, there was a sound so loud I thought I had chipped a tooth. I freaked out, calling for Mark to wake up and come into the kitchen immediately. Did I have some new brain damage? The panic from that event put me in bed for the rest of the day on Ativan. All because of cereal.

It was a huge production to be home. Someone needed to be with me at all times. I spent most of my days whiling away the hours sitting at the same spot on my couch, which became discolored from my using it as a table for food, drinks, and snacks, with a new indentation mirroring the shape of my ass. My afternoons became reruns of *Magnum, P.I.*

As the days wore on, I created various methods to cope with the painstakingly slow pace of recovery.

Foggy-headedness became a companion that refused to leave.

Nothing seemed real. I'd sit on the couch and look at the furniture in my living room every morning thinking it looked fake, blurry, strange, just like the hallway in rehab had when I first ventured out from my room. I was in dire need of a coping mechanism to combat this feeling of utter strangeness.

I had to rationalize living with this feeling. I had to come up with a way to stop myself from thinking I had permanent brain damage. I formulated a plan. I would tell myself I been bonked in the head. Maybe it was a football that hit me during a game and I was waiting for a concussion to go away. I didn't care that the story wasn't true, anything to help me adjust to that feeling of detachment from reality I had.

Every night, I continued to call out "Dizzy!" as I made my attempts to fall asleep. It was punishing but less torturous than it had been in the hospital.

It went on like this for months. I would be fine during the day and at night my fears would rise up again. *What if my blood pressure is too high? What if I have another stroke?* I was terrified that anything I did would give me another stroke, that I'd end up even more paralyzed, or even die. While my friends were out for dinner or at a gig or just enjoying life, I was at home measuring my pupil size and taking my blood pressure.

These were the trenches of stroke recovery. I had heard stories about people who survived catastrophic injuries and were recovering, but I had never known what "recovering" really meant. I had always thought recovery meant sitting in bed watching reruns of *Sanford and Son* or eating chicken soup on the couch. Oh, how wrong I was! "Recovery" translated into enduring terrible anxiety-producing experiences while my brain slowly healed itself and reestablished those neural connections. Every second felt like an eternity.

Outpatient rehab—speech, occupational and physical therapies— began the first week I was home. Mark drove me to every appointment. I went to the outpatient center in my wheelchair, feeling like I'd climbed Mt. Everest just by getting from the garage parking lot to the front door. I wore loose-fitting clothes, a baseball cap, my orthopedic-looking sneakers, an outdated (1990s-style) fanny pack, and my black prescription sunglasses to soften the glare.

I was a mess when I first began outpatient therapy, constantly asking the same questions: "Will I ever be normal again? Will I always have a limp? Will I ever wear heels again?" Basically, I was a red lipstick-wearing pain in the ass.

I was quite a case for my therapy team. I was highly physically impaired. I was terrified of moving my neck. And then, of course, there were those pesky questions. But despite my apparent unease, I was eager to do whatever exercises they threw at me. I wanted to prove I could do it. And I quickly bonded with my new therapists. Seeing them became the highlight of my day.

My physical therapist was a young woman named Sara. Sara encouraged me to do things I never thought I could. At first, we focused on balancing against the table without hands and riding the recumbent bicycle. Later, we walked across the therapy room with me using just my cane. I had a slight stroke limp. It's a distinctive kind of limp, where the paralyzed leg juts out, swinging to the side in a circular motion with every step. I was determined to get rid of it, to get out of those orthopedic sneakers and into heels again. Dancing onstage in heels again one day was a lofty goal, but it was my goal. I refused to consider any other possibility.

With Sara's help it wasn't long before I ditched the wheelchair for good and walked using my cane and leg brace. I was weak still and unbalanced, but I could do it. Sara encouraged me to believe in myself and not backslide into the comfort of my wheelchair. She encouraged me to take things a step further, always pushing me toward achievement and never doubting my capabilities. It was a long way off, but the thought of walking without assistance and without a limp — or even running — excited me.

One day, Sara told me to bring in some of my shoes. "We're going to practice walking in heels," she said. I think I gasped in excitement.

The next day, I brought in three pair of shoes: my leopard wedges, my platform sandals, and my retro rockabilly-style block heels. I don't think that's what Sara had in mind when she told me to bring in my shoes — she was probably thinking one pair of small conservative heeled shoes, maybe. Not me. I was dressing for a dance club. I wobbled across the physical therapy room while Sara kept a watchful eye on my every move and remained by my side in case I lost my balance.

Jerry was my speech therapist, a wonderful guy who made me genuinely enjoy speech therapy for the first time. We played games, we worked on identifying tones and repeating them back, we talked about life.

My occupational therapist, Nicole, was friendly, compassionate, and very patient. I had very little motion in my left arm or hand and could only raise my arm a few degrees. All of the fingers on my left hand, except for my pinky, were often balled in a fist from increased muscle tone. And I couldn't move my neck at all. I was so protective of my neck that I refused to do any exercises that required me to engage any muscles in the upper half of my body. Nicole had endless patience with me and always made me feel at ease. We often chatted about our lives as she guided me through hand and arm exercises.

The head-spinning was gradually decreasing each day, but I still had the brain fog that felt like someone had hit me over the head with a frying pan (or knocked me out with a football). We had our work cut out for us.

Nicole had me do exercises like trying to hold a cup in my left hand and bringing it to my mouth. I usually spilled the water on the floor. I grabbed brightly colored blocks with my left hand and put them in a bin, one by one. Nicole tried teaching me to put on a bra, but I couldn't do it. We tried to put my hair in a ponytail, and I couldn't do that either. (Enter the baseball cap.) In too many ways, I was a prisoner in my own body.

Nicole suggested some products for disabled people, believing this might help me at home. I didn't want that. I told her I was getting back to normal so I wouldn't need them. I constantly told her I was going to be one hundred percent normal again. She often took note of my feisty attitude and had faith that I was going to conquer this stroke. We bonded right away. She truly cared about each of her patients and treated them like old friends.

I joined an online support group for young stroke survivors, and often read posts by people encouraging us to accept our fate. They said it was okay to grieve for the old you.

I couldn't grieve for the old me. My perception of myself was what mattered most, despite how I looked or whether or not I needed a wheelchair, a walker or a cane, and I didn't see myself as disabled. The old me was in there trying to find a way out of this situation.

Still, I felt a kinship with everyone who used a wheelchair or other mobility aid. We weren't "handicapped." We weren't "disabled." We were "differently abled." We had a different perspective on life. Living life in a wheelchair opens your eyes to what you would otherwise take for granted.

I decided to look online for stroke survivors in later stages of their recovery. I found Peter Coghlan, a young stroke survivor in Australia who had a brain stem stroke like mine. Peter got something worse, something called "locked-in syndrome," which meant that his entire body was paralyzed, everything except for his eyelids.

At first Peter communicated using an alphabet board. Now, he was walking and talking as if nothing had happened. He had a landscape business and worked outdoors in the sun. I looked at his videos and read his blog many times over the next months. His story gave me hope. His refusal to give up inspires me to do the same. Peter and I have become great friends.

Every week I noticed small improvements in walking or using my hand. Eventually, I started carrying my cane but not relying on it. Mark took me one day to a local farmers market and to a store and I walked without my cane. Then I took a short walk with my cousin Brooke, mostly carrying my cane. I felt free.

Sadly, I paid a hefty price for my five minutes of freedom. Within hours of my outing I began to get a severe pain in my good leg. I couldn't leave the bed or cross my legs. That evening, I was in so much pain it took two people, my mother and Mark, to transfer me to the wheelchair, which I had to revert to using.

It was an awful setback, and I don't suffer setbacks lightly. I had made so much progress, and I was back to square one!

Mark took me to the ER at Mass General. It was terrifying to be back. I told the check-in nurse that I was a stroke patient, and I was promptly whisked to the front of the queue and given every test imaginable on my leg. To my relief, the doctors determined that I did not have a blood clot in my leg and I was free to go home.

The hellish pain intensified that evening. Even the slightest gentle brushing of a bed sheet touching my calf felt like an anvil had been dropped on my leg. Mark took me back to ER.

Mark fell asleep in my wheelchair as I lay in the ER bed attempting to get some sleep. Every few minutes, I was awakened to the sounds of him rolling out of the room and into the hall in a deep sleep. It was like something out of a Carol Burnett skit. I had to whisper-yell, "Mark! Get back here! You're rolling into the hall!"

During this ER visit, I was not a priority as it had been determined earlier that day that I wasn't having a stroke. Twelve sleepless hours later, I was sent home with a walker to use for the next couple of weeks. I had simply pulled a hamstring, but I was so incredibly sensitive to touch and pain it felt like a tank was rolling over my leg if I even touched my skin there with a tissue. I went home the next morning.

At this point, I was still dressing like an extra from the cast of *The Golden Girls*. I was like Estelle Getty with a walker. When I was in public, people stared with empathy and wonderment: what the hell had happened to that young woman? Why is she using a walker? I even overheard healthy-looking elderly people making hushed comments about me. Families avoided me in restaurants, taking a seat at a table farther away, as if they could catch it or something. I wanted to say to these people, *I didn't think young people could have strokes either, but here I am.*

I started to change my appearance. I was strong enough to make an effort to look good. I wore my hair pushed to one side. I wore earrings and full makeup. Sometimes I dressed for therapy in my shredded punk sweaters, big jewelry, high-topped sneakers, and leopard leggings. It made a huge difference in how I felt and was worth the extra effort.

Before the stroke, I could shop in the mall all day. I longed to go to the local mall, to shop aimlessly, wander around and visit all the stores. But I was afraid of public places. The sounds, the people, the escalators, even the hard floors scared me. What if I fell? One fall could destroy all my progress. I had forgotten how to use an escalator. Just looking at the moving stairs frightened me.

My mother took me to a local mall before it opened for the day's business, when it was filled with senior citizens who were also there walking for exercise. I had to become familiar with being in public again and learn how to navigate my way around people and things like clothing racks and shoe displays. We did this together for weeks, just going to the mall before it opened. I knew it was an important first step.

Grocery shopping was a similar problem. Mark took me to

a market near our house, a place I had been to no fewer than a thousand times over the past several years since we bought our house. I started to panic as I walked through the aisles with him. There were so many items, and the shelves seemed to close in on me as I tried to choose a jar of pickles. Overwhelming. "Let's get out of here," I said, and we were out of there, returning to the parked car, where I could calm down in the safety of the passenger's seat. Abrupt exits during a shopping trip became the norm for me.

My mother offered to take me to a beauty supply store. I could get lost in that kind of store for hours. I was so excited, it was like Christmas in September. At the store, I looked at the hair accessories for maybe ten minutes — and then it started again. I was overstimulated by the array of hair elastics and the general sounds of the store. Customers were talking and music was playing in the background. It was all too much for my brain to handle. My palms were wet with sweat. I had trouble catching my breath. I looked at my mother and started to fall into her, unable to stand for another second. She caught me and a salesgirl found me a chair. After five minutes, I regained my bearings enough to walk to the exit.

Over time, the more I was in public, the easier it became to adjust to all the stimulation. Exposure was key. I tried to do something in public every day, even if I only lasted five minutes. Soon I was able to withstand hours of being in public in loud or crowded spaces. In rehab, Sara fashioned a mock escalator by placing an exercise stepper behind a treadmill. I walked on the machine holding into the side bars and facing backwards, pretending I was getting off at the dress department in Macy's. It worked. I became accustomed to the motion of an escalator and didn't fear falling next time I stepped onto one.

I could go shopping with a friend, I could go to the market and help with choosing groceries, I could buy new makeup or hair jewelry at the beauty supply shop, and Mark and I could have dinner at a favorite neighborhood restaurant. This was the ordinary becoming extraordinary, and I was grateful for every new step.

Chapter Seventeen

WHEN MARK JOINED ME AS a law partner in 2013, we had high hopes of creating a successful, busy firm. I had a steady stream of bankruptcy and criminal clients and Mark was hoping to develop a corporate law clientele. With Mark busy in his role as my full-time caregiver and personal driver, the entire business came to a screeching halt after my stroke. In fact, my law practice all but disappeared. Mark visited the office a few times while I was in the hospital and at rehab, but his activities were limited to things like making a few phone calls or drafting documents for our existing cases since caring for his wife had become a full-time job.

My office was in shambles. The Friday before my stroke I was preparing for a trial scheduled to take place the following week. Books were open to the page I was last reading. A half-empty plastic water bottle sat on the corner of the crowded desk.

Files were stacked on my desk exactly as I had left them on Friday, May 30, when I'd left to attend funeral services for someone who had (ironically) died of a stroke a few days before. It was an eerie time capsule, everything sitting undisturbed until Mark eventually found the time to clean it up. It was as if time stopped that Friday on the last weekend in May.

Mark and I knew that one of us had to work, and it certainly wasn't going to be me. I couldn't even imagine how I would ever resume my law practice the way things looked right now.

A few weeks after my return home, Mark and I decided that he would return to the office and do what he could to salvage our business. My mother and Mark's mother, who visited me nearly every day, would take turns being my babysitters while Mark spent the day at our office, since I couldn't be left alone. I imagined he felt liberated to finally be doing something besides waiting on me or wheeling me into the bathroom.

As for the housecleaning, our mothers, two women in their sixties and seventies, took care of things while I sat helplessly by. There was nothing I could do but watch as our dishes piled up in the sink, laundry grew into high piles, and pieces of rehab equipment cluttered our once-immaculate living room.

As our mothers folded my laundry on one of their babysitting days, I decided this nonsense had to stop. I at least had to start dressing myself. I was not going to continue as a toddler in the self-care department. From then on I became resolute about dressing myself with no help from anyone. It took some extreme maneuvering just to force my left hand through the armholes of my new, extra-large, short-sleeved T-shirts. I gazed longingly at the clothes hanging in my closet, wishing for even a glimmer of hope for wearing something attractive again.

Patience, I reminded myself.

It took fifteen minutes to get my socks on. To clasp my bra, I had to twist the back of the bra around to the front of my body and use my right hand to clasp the hook, then push it around to the back and presto! I was wearing a bra. Putting my loose-fitting elastic waistband pants on over the leg brace and getting my left arm through the sleeve of those T-shirts involved a lot of swearing and grunting, but I could say I dressed myself. I didn't need my husband or my mother to dress me.

During my hours on the living room couch, I read articles about neuroplasticity, which gave me hope for relearning basic skills. Certain kinds of games, I found out, strengthen the mind, which in turn strengthens the connections between the brain and paralyzed limbs. I became addicted to the online game site called Lumosity, which strengthens cognitive abilities. In the Lumosity games I could be a barista or a waitress at a busy café,

I could be a pet detective or a train conductor, all from the comfort of my laptop. My type A personality was right there with it, eager to raise my Lumosity score. I wasn't used to scoring in a low percentile, and being one-handed meant that I was slow. A perfect challenge! I could compete against other game subscribers, or at least feel like I was competing, and that helped push me to improve.

Each week, I had more freedom. The late summer days remained long, giving me the sense I had more time to make myself try new things. Attempting to brush my teeth with my left hand was quite an endeavor. With my right hand, I pushed the toothbrush into my left, which tended to curl into a fist position at times. I did my best to move the toothbrush up and down against my teeth, creating a mess of drooling toothpaste. Not bad, I'd tell myself, as I put everything away when I was done.

Eating was an adventure and something I took pride in doing on my own; that feeding bit with the bib had to be retired just as soon as possible. With my left hand, I cut the food on my plate, hoping I wouldn't stab myself with the knife. Then, awkward as it was, I proceeded to eat using my left hand. Brushing my hair was even harder as I didn't have the strength in my left hand to run the brush through my hair. I frequently relied on the baseball cap to take care of things when I went out. These are the sorts of things—the dailies—you don't think about when all your parts are working. I wished for that luxury of ease again someday.

And as the hot summer days ended, my wish came true, or rather, *one* of my wishes did. My dizziness slowly dissipated. It was a miracle! Imagine loud music playing—loud *raucous* music playing—nonstop for twelve weeks or so and then gradually everything goes quiet. Perfectly, beautifully quiet. I could sleep better without the dizziness, I could see better without it, I could walk better. There wasn't anything I couldn't do better without having to deal with that swirl inside my head. The disappearance of the dizziness was a sign that I was really defeating this stroke.

To celebrate (and because department stores still overwhelmed me with their abundance of choices), I ordered a few pieces of sexy clothing online. I went to see Candice, my hair colorist, and asked for fiery red streaks to be put in my hair, as I had often done over the past few years. Whenever I went out, even if it was just to a doctor's appointment, I put on a pair of earrings and one of my trendy looking outfits. I often wore my faux leather leggings, or my thigh-high leopard print flat boots. I wore sweaters with zippers and anything else I could that looked hip. I was sick of those oversized T-shirts and I didn't care anymore how long it took to get dressed. I had more dexterity, too, which meant I could open and close the button on my skinny jeans again. I can't even begin to imagine what the clinic staff thought of the woman who came in for her blood draw looking like a backup dancer for Madonna.

I enjoyed being a performer, and now that the dizziness was gone, I decided that if anyone could turn this not-so-pretty dance into a Hollywood-style affair, it was going to be me. I had graduated from a wheelchair to a cane and a brace, and whenever I could I walked holding my cane horizontally, at the ready if I needed it. If I was going to ride this crazy train, I was going to do it in style.

My facial droop was also improving. It had been rather slight to begin with, but I was always very self-conscious about it. It only seemed to be noticeable when Mark took a few candid photos of me on his iPhone. As the days wore on, the droop gradually disappeared and I recognized myself again. I remembered that neuropsychologist in rehab, Dr. Montague. When I had asked him if my droop would ever go away, hoping to hear "Of course it will!", he alluded to the possibility that I wouldn't get my face back. "That's probably the best you're going to get," he said. I was saddened and annoyed and my eyes filled with tears—what a prospect!—but in my heart, I didn't fully believe him. Now I knew for certain I could trust my heart.

September passed with cooling temperatures and shortening days, and October came and went with the quicker pace I was getting used to and definitely preferred.

Progress was slow where my hand and leg were concerned, and I still didn't know what I could expect from my voice. I didn't have full control over my voice, so I frequently wavered in a high-pitched tone anytime I practiced.

Soon I had a real turning point, an eye-opening, startling and joyous experience in the most unlikely of places. I visited a neuro-ophthalmologist at Mass General, dressed that day in my Red Sox leather jacket, my skinny jeans, my baseball hat, and my high-topped sneakers. I looked like I was going to grab a burger at the Cask and Flagon near Fenway Park, not going to a doctor appointment. I had brought my wheelchair as I needed it for navigating the humongous hospital. Mark was with me, but I told him I'd go by myself to use the restroom while he stayed in the waiting room. I left my wheelchair behind, choosing instead to carefully walk about fifty feet to the handicapped restroom. I was a little slow using the restroom, but I figured that was alright since no one had been in line waiting for it. When I finished and opened the door, I was greeted by an elderly woman holding a cane. She stared at me with a look of disdain. She must have arrived after I'd gone inside and was maddened to have had to wait for someone she perceived as being perfectly able-bodied.

It was a defining day in my recovery. I walked back to the waiting room giddy with excitement. My stroke was undetectable! That cantankerous woman who gave me the stink-eye for using a handicapped restroom had given me a gigantic gift.

Chapter Eighteen

RESUMING EVERYDAY ACTIVITIES GAVE ME the mental uplift I craved so intensely, but the fact that I still couldn't sing or play my violin because of the injury to my neck was like rubbing salt in a colossal wound.

My vocal injury was difficult to explain to anyone who has not personally experienced that same thing. While my speaking voice had for months sounded like I had a mouthful of marbles, the stroke didn't render me unable to speak. I sounded weak, hoarse and took frequent breaths while speaking, but otherwise I communicated clearly to nearly everyone who I came into contact with. So, on the surface, my voice seemed okay to most people and the gravity of my musical losses were not readily apparent.

I had read about famous contemporary singers like Adele, Celine Dion, and Steven Tyler. They'd had vocal problems and couldn't sing for a time. Some even had surgery. When their vocal cords healed, they went right back to singing and making records.

I was different. I had lost the *ability* to sing. It was nothing that rest alone would cure. Seeing how much progress I'd made physically, friends would ask if I planned to return to singing. It was understandable. Logically, I should have been able to jump right back into singing, like a kid who gets back on her bicycle after falling off. But it wasn't that easy. My brain didn't know how to sing anymore, and resting my voice wasn't a solution like it was for those other singers.

All of my vocal abilities vanished into thin air when that blood clot hit my brain. The skills that had taken me a lifetime to acquire were simply gone. For me, the ability to hold a note, to have a smooth tone and good pitch, to perform a modulating vibrato or sing a vocal run, even to regulate my volume, all of these qualities of a professional singer were buried somewhere inside a brain that was busy battling its way back from a stroke.

Something else the stroke took away was my ability to play musical instruments, or most of them, anyway. This was another vicious blow. My instrument for so much of my youth was the violin. I was only somewhat competent on the violin, but I didn't care. I had a few guitars, I played some harmonica, I bought a piano and learned to play it, and more recently, I played the melodica. I loved to be surrounded by music, making sounds and melodies.

At this point, in order to successfully play any of those, I needed a functional left hand. Playing the violin required the use of my left hand to finger the notes while my right hand and arm bowed the instrument. The only instrument I could play singlehandedly, albeit one lonely chord at a time, was the piano.

Having this illness strip away my ability to play a musical instrument that had been part of my life for thirty years was not part of my recovery plan. I decided one day to take things in hand (so to speak!).

I sat at my piano and played the melody to the Nat King Cole hit, "Nature Boy." It took so much energy to get onto the piano bench, read the sheet music, and simultaneously play the melody with just my right hand, that after one verse I had to lie down. It was hard to believe that before the stroke I had played piano with both hands for hours on end while singing. *Hours.*

I didn't dare touch the violin. I wasn't sure if my left hand could even finger the strings. And I didn't want to put the tension on my neck and wasn't about to push things for the sake of maybe getting a couple of notes. Fear flew in my face again: *What if it gives me another stroke?*

The cello is in the same orchestral family of instruments as the violin, each having four strings and each played in a similar fashion, with a bow. I thought the cello produced a richer sound than the violin, I couldn't hurt my neck playing it, and I decided I wanted to give it a try. A childhood friend named Gary heard about this. Gary knew I could no longer play the violin and that I had lost my singing voice and how devastating it was. He restored instruments as a hobby and wanted to do something to bring a bit of musical happiness to me.

One day Gary walked through my front door with a surprise for me. He carried a gorgeous purple cello he had restored himself. "When I heard about your stroke," he said, "I wanted to make you smile in even the smallest way. Giving you this cello is my way of bringing some sunshine to your life."

Such a beautiful instrument! Such a beautiful gift. And such a kind and generous man to want to do this for me. I thanked Gary profusely and promised I would learn to play it.

That night, I gave it a good try. I could scarcely move the fingers on my left hand, and that was necessary to play the instrument. I also couldn't bear weight with my fingers on the cello's thin wooden neck. With my weak hand I pressed down on the strings with enough force to finally make a screechy sound when I bowed with the right hand. I was no Yo-Yo Ma, but I could do it. I had a chance, anyway.

⚜ ⚜

My hand needed more therapy, a lot of it, if I was ever going to seriously attempt a musical instrument again. Nicole, my occupational therapist, recommended me for an appointment with a representative for a company called Bioness. Bioness develops and manufactures systems for the rehabilitation of physical impairments resulting from central nervous system disorders, and I fit the bill.

I met a representative from Bioness at Spaulding Rehab, and he demonstrated an electronic device that stimulated the hand and arm muscles. I was amazed! With something like jolts of electrical current whizzing through my hand in a pulsating, almost rhythmic pattern, the device would make my fingers twitch and straighten.

I tried it on, activating the voltage for a few minutes, and then I took it off. My arm and hand muscles were loose, almost back to normal! "Are you serious?" I shouted, absolutely floored by what I was seeing.

"It takes some time," the rep said, with a smile. "But you can see the possibilities."

In about three minutes, my left arm and hand had reverted to their quasi-paralyzed and stiff state. But it was three minutes of bliss! For three full minutes I was able to move my arm freely without it being tight and spastic and feeling like it weighed five hundred pounds.

I bought the unit and I used it faithfully every day. I used it while watching TV, giving my arm and hand the electrical stimulation and relishing the few minutes of normalcy I got when I removed it from my arm. Gradually, a few minutes turned into thirty minutes, and by Easter the next year (2015) my arm and hand were almost returned to functioning normally. I had only a little tightness in my hand when making a fist; most of my fingers moved freely. My left index finger remained stubborn and liked to curl a bit. Otherwise, it was as if the stroke had never affected my arm or hand.

During my days in rehab, I decided to write a book about my stroke experience. I wanted to inspire others who faced seemingly insurmountable feats and conquered them, but first, I had to conquer my own. I knew there was hope for recovery, no matter how bleak things seemed. Human beings are resilient. If by modeling it I could motivate and inspire someone to reclaim his or her life, this entire stroke experience would have served a purpose.

Of course, the challenges of one-handed writing were daunting. Yet, I was determined to write a book about this even if I only had one hand and even if I typed one word per minute.

When I was back home again I continued with my one-handed typing. I squeezed a tiny rubber ball in the shape of a starfish every day for hours, and played Jenga with my young cousin Brooke, slowly constructing a wooden tower that would eventually topple over so we could start all over again. Anything to exercise my hands. I made pancake shapes from putty and passed empty sheboxes back and forth with Mark using both hands. And now, I owned the crème de la crème of therapy devices, my treasured Bioness Arm.

After several weeks of using what I called my "bionic arm," I could type more freely using two hands again, instead of having a rigid left hand moving about wildly on my keyboard as I tried to type with my right. I played piano with two hands, too, making a full chord with my left hand. For the first time since the stroke I could sit at the piano and write music, picking up where I left off at the end of May. It was as if I had never stopped.

A few days before my stroke, my good friend, Grammy Award-winning composer and pianist Laura Sullivan, contacted me about a new video she was producing called "900 Voices." She thought it would be great if I could be a part of the project. After the stroke stole my singing voice, I thought Laura would never want me to be part of this project. I was wrong.

Laura was very concerned about me when she read about my stroke on social media. She lives in California, but sent me messages and flowers while I was in rehab. She contacted me a couple of months after the stroke to tell me she still wanted me to be in the video, if I was willing. Was I! Now that I could play the piano with two hands and everything was starting to feel so much more natural, I knew that participating in this video would be a huge milestone in my recovery and my return to singing.

It seemed a simple task. I would sing the word "love" on one note. Nothing fancy.

But singing the word "love" on one note turned out to be anything but simple. It took every ounce of physical energy I had and many weeks of rehearsing before I could give Laura a one-minute video clip of me singing that one word in one note. And I still had no vibrato. But I could do it, and the sound was smooth for those few moments. Laura said she loved it.

When I watched the clip I gave to Laura, I saw myself on video for the first time since my stroke. I was wearing my "Stroke Survivor" shirt like a badge of honor, and my leather pants. Only months before, I was in a bed in the ICU unable to see clearly, swallow, or move, with no singing voice. Now I was singing in a music video. I was alive and kicking and excited for the world to see that I was determined to make a comeback.

Laura gave me the springboard I needed to jump-start my singing voice. She saw me as her friend Valerie, the vocalist, not the poor girl who had a stroke. In fact, every one of my colleagues at The Recording Academy (the Grammy organization) treated me like a professional musician throughout this entire ordeal. They were shocked and saddened to hear what happened to me, but they spoke to me as if nothing had changed. I was still the professional singer. Their treatment of me helped my psyche immensely. If I was made to feel like a musician, it was easy to act like one. If I could act like one, it meant my voice was desirable. And if I felt desirable, everything I lost had the potential to return that much quicker. State of mind is a powerful thing.

People may view this behavior toward me as insignificant, but as a newly "differently-abled" person, it meant far more than I can express. When something as mind-shattering as a paralyzing stroke hits, it can be easy to dive into despair, pining for the return of the way things used to be. Feelings of sheer worthlessness can creep in quicker than a New York minute. But when someone treats you as if you still matter, when they recognize that the real you is still the same, there is a sense of jubilation and the knowledge that one day you will return to doing the things you love and the stroke will be inconsequential. And that is worth its weight in gold.

Chapter Nineteen

I T WAS NOVEMBER 2014, FIVE months after the stroke. The day had arrived that I could finally send that email to my friends in Italy, the email I had written so long ago, when its message was still a dream. I typed the words in Italian, proudly declaring that I was no longer paralyzed on my left side, I was back to singing, and I planned to attend the Umbria Jazz Clinics in Perugia, Italy, again, in 2015. It felt fantastic to hit the "send" button.

Most days, I walked a mile, without a brace or cane, and I wasn't even tired afterward. I still had a slight limp, but I was determined to change that.

I watched Mark and my therapists and noted how they walked. I studied my legs and how they moved. I practiced on my daily walks, focusing not on walking but on keeping my left leg straight so it didn't jut out to the side with every step. I used all the energy I had. Sara, my physical therapist, taught me to use the rehab treadmill watching the mirror, so I could look at my legs walking. We did this a few times each week. We walked constantly, at different speeds, through the physical therapy room. We balanced between bars, we ran laps weaving through an agility ladder, we walked up and down stairs, all while timing my speed so I could beat my own progress the next week.

In November, Mark started giving me little hints about my Christmas present, saying I'd never be able to guess what it was. He likes to surprise me, and I knew he was planning something big.

"You have to use Skype," he said with a silly grin.

Skype? I only Skyped before with a few friends overseas. I figured it was probably a little joke from my brother-in-law in Bangkok; he was a professional comedian. Granted, I am grateful for any gift I receive, but I wasn't quite in the mood for dancing Thai marionettes or a comedy monologue, and I guessed this was what my "gift" was going to involve.

Nevertheless, that morning in November I logged onto Skype and my friend Ilaria appeared on my screen. I missed her so much! Ilaria had emailed me every day since the stroke and was so sad she wasn't able to be with me through those horridly tough times.

I started to cry at the sight of her face on the screen. She was working at her family's B&B in Venice, she said, and she had taken a ceramic horse from the hotel lobby. Excited, she held it up to the screen and announced that it was my gift. I don't particularly care for ceramic animals, yet I cried with happiness just knowing she was on the other end of the screen. I hadn't seen her in all these months. "Thank you! What a beautiful gift!", I shouted excitedly at the screen through my tears.

Then she held up an airline ticket. "Do you see this? I'm coming to see you in December! I was only kidding with that ceramic horse from the lobby!"

"You what?" I cried even harder.

Mark had bought Ilaria a round-trip airline ticket from Venice to Boston because she wanted to be with me during my recovery.

It was the best Christmas present I had ever received. Ilaria was coming to see me!

Mark sacrificed so many months to take care of me day and night, catering to my every possible need twenty-four hours a day. Now, he was going even further, bringing my dear friend Ilaria to me! He is an amazing husband and I am lucky to have him in my life.

Before her arrival, I planned a lot of activities for Ilaria to do with me on this trip, her first, to the United States. I wanted it to be a memorable one for her, although she would have been happy just to spend the week in my living room.

I was at therapy on my way to the restroom and busy counting the days until my dear friend's arrival when I had a setback I never could have seen coming. I tripped over my sneaker and fell headfirst onto the wooden floor, cracking my forehead open. Blood poured out like a river.

The moment I lost my footing, I knew I was going down. It was as if my world was moving in slow motion. I knew it was going to be a hard blow, but I had no time to prevent my fall and nothing close enough to hold on to. So I released all tension in my body and allowed myself to freely fall, suffering a blow so hard I was dizzy on contact. I screamed and sobbed uncontrollably while the entire staff rushed to my aid.

"My progress! It's gone! Everything I've done for months is out the window!" I wailed, crying a river of tears red with blood.

Sara, who had been tending to another patient in the gym, saw what was happening. She grabbed every towel in sight and ran to me to soak up the blood. The gash in my forehead was two inches wide.

"Will I be okay?" I asked Sara, shaking and weeping. I hadn't been this terrified since the night of my stroke.

"Of course you will!" she exclaimed, as she desperately worked to stop the bleeding until the paramedics arrived. My clothes, my shoes, my hands and face, even my hair was covered with blood.

Paramedics rushed me to emergency, where I was immediately given a CT scan to check for bleeding in my brain. My blood was thin from the blood-thinning medication and I was at risk for a brain hemorrhage, which I was afraid would kill me.

A brain injury on top of a brain injury? The first one likely the result of turning my neck too quickly, this one caused by tripping over my sneaker simply walking from the waiting room to the bathroom.

Absurd.

How was this fair? In my legal work, I had seen the worst of humanity, criminals who spent much of their lives stealing, taking drugs, being violent and harming others, and *they* were okay. And here I destroyed myself first by turning my neck and, next, tripping on a sneaker. I had been focused on fighting to get my life back for months and doing things that had seemed impossible. I was strong and passionate and driven to beat the stroke.

Something was truly unconscionable about the whole situation.

The CT scan came back with good news. There was no bleeding in my brain, and besides needing stitches to close the wound on my forehead, I was fine. "We're giving you several stitches in your forehead, and you'll have two black eyes for a week," the doctor said, while a nurse stood at the side of my hospital bed, dressing my newly stitched forehead with a bandage. "But you're going to be okay."

You're going to be okay.

I let those words repeat in my head over and over. *You're going to be okay.*

Yet again I had narrowly escaped a life-threatening situation.

Despite my gratefulness to be alive, a sense of despair washed over me. I halted my daily exercise routine and lay in bed for most of two weeks. I ached all over from the fall. I wasn't sure how to bear this, the uncertainty involved with every step. Now when I did walk, I walked slowly and hesitantly. I used a cane again, worried that any move could result in another fall. Even my voice sounded weaker when I spoke.

Ilaria arrived in Boston in mid-December, two weeks after my fall. I had a fresh scar on my forehead and a swollen face with puffy eyes. I looked like I'd been in a fistfight and wound up on the losing end.

But Ilaria didn't care. She helped me see that I had to keep going, I had a responsibility to keep going, to myself and to others. I had come so far in such a short time. Every time I said a word about my singing career being over, she wasted no time in correcting me.

"You are *still* a talented singer!" she told me, with her beautiful Italian accent. I desperately wanted to believe her.

Ilaria and I spent the week doing things I hadn't done since my stroke. She never left my side. We saw "A Christmas Carol" at a local theater, seated in my wheelchair. I hadn't been to a theater since the stroke and wondered if I could handle the bright lights, loud sounds, and the crowd of people. Thankfully, I could — special lights, sound effects, all of it. Three months earlier I would have had to take Ativan to make it through.

Just knowing Ilaria was right there with me, believing in me, encouraging me to try new things, gave me the push I needed to get back into the world. That week, we went out to dinner many times. Ilaria and I went Christmas shopping with my parents; it was the first time I'd been shopping since June. We visited a museum and toured Boston's Public Garden.

Fear, I realized, was the only thing holding me back from doing the things I had always loved to do. Once I let go of the fear, I began to live normally again. I went to crowded public places — the mall, museums — and pushed myself to walk even farther than what I had been doing for the last few months. It had taken this long, but at last I had realized my only limitations were the ones I placed on myself.

Chapter Twenty

S ARA HAD SOMETHING NEW FOR me one day in January. She could see that although my resolve was there, since my fall I was frustrated, my walk was slower, a lot more hesitant, and limpy again. The sound of my speaking voice was low, hushed. I felt like I'd taken ten steps backwards.

"Valerie," she said one morning, "I want you to try something. Something I know you can do."

I couldn't imagine what it could be. What could I try that I hadn't tried already?

Did she want me to get on a bike and take a ride by the Charles River on a Sunday afternoon to see how my agility training was paying off?

No, my physical therapist wanted me to try rock climbing.

What? She couldn't be serious.

I had never rock climbed in my life, and she wanted me to do it while recovering from a stroke? "Think about it," Sara said. "And let me know next week."

Rock climbing? It seemed crazy! I was skittish about heights, on top of everything else.

But the more I thought about it, the more I realized rock climbing was exactly the kind of crazy I relished. If I could rock climb eight months after a devastating stroke, I could show the world that stroke is not a death sentence and that people are capable of a full comeback if they are given the opportunity. Maybe someone else suffering from a stroke or from another illness would see me do this and be encouraged to shine.

I couldn't wait to do it.

A few weeks later I walked into a local YMCA and was immediately struck by the sight of an indoor rock-climbing wall. Sara met me there, and Mark watched from the perimeter with my friend Rossana.

Sara greeted me. "You're here!"

"I told you I would be," I laughed. "You know I'm a little nervous about this whole rock-climbing thing. Someone is going to be helping me on the wall, right? I am not a fan of heights, that's for sure! "Sara linked her arm in mine. "You're going to be fine. Come on. I want you to meet the trainer."

As the trainer strapped me into the harness, which ran around my waist and between my legs and hooked together with a clasp I inspected carefully after he closed it, I wondered how I was going to accomplish this. My left side was still weak, yet I had to propel myself up the side of the wall like Spider-Man while not looking down for any reason whatsoever.

I couldn't believe I was doing this. It was surreal. And trust me, you never get used to surreal.

I scaled the face of the wall, grasping the protruding "rocks" (small artificial pieces) with my hands and stepping on them with both feet. Feet that couldn't walk not too long ago. A left foot that had been limp and lifeless. I felt like the ultimate badass.

With my right hand secured on the plastic handhold in my reach, I pushed with my good leg, hoping my left leg would follow suit. It did. I clenched both hands like claws, holding onto each handhold as if it was a life preserver. Step after step, I climbed higher. I was weak and slow, and I didn't reach the top of the wall, but I climbed halfway there. And to think, just weeks before I was lying in a pool of blood after a forward fall threatened to steal my recovery. And not very long before that I was completely paralyzed on my left side, constantly dizzy, and seeing double. Simply rolling onto my side made me almost pass out from out-of-control dizziness. Now, I was flailing about while spinning off a rock-climbing wall with no hint of vertigo. At one point, I turned to face Sara, who watched from below, and I was sent spinning in circles in my harness for a few moments. Oh my

142

God, I thought. This is it. I am going to get dizzy and vomit. But, nothing happened. I didn't even get dizzy.

Around the same time as that amazing adventure, Sara arranged for aquatic therapy at their indoor pool in Charlestown. In the water, I moved almost naturally. My left leg moved freely. My arms and hands were fluid, not stiff. I ran for the first time since the stroke. I was in a harness under water, but I was actually running!

Back at my regular therapy session, I told Sara I wanted to learn to run again, outside the water. Before the stroke I didn't particularly care for running. My running experience was limited to a few minutes on my treadmill or running to catch a train during law school. Now I couldn't get enough of it. I missed being *able* to do it.

I don't think Sara ever said no to me. That day, she strapped me into a harness connected to a treadmill and on a very slow speed at first, and taught me how to run again. I felt like a stuntwoman on *MacGyver*. To see myself running, even in a harness in the rehab mirror, told me I was doing it. I was conquering this stroke.

Nothing was going to halt my momentum. My setbacks — the pulled hamstring, the head-splitting fall — were not going to make me fail. They were rocks on the climbing wall. They were the gatekeepers on the way to the top, where the shining jewels lay in wait for my claim. I was an athlete of sorts, and I treated my recovery as intense athletic training. I was focused on returning to my pre-stroke state, but I realized I could be even better if I worked hard enough. Forget the story I once had to tell myself to be able to accept my perpetually foggy mind. I was never hit in the head with a football and recovering from a concussion. I had survived a brain stem stroke and I was recovering all of who I ever was, and gaining even more. I was ready to charge through the rest of my recovery like it was an Olympic event and I was set to take home a gold medal.

That evening, as I lay in my bed surfing the Internet, I learned about an Italian teenager named Beatrice (Bebe) Vio. Bebe is one of the best wheelchair fencers in the world. With no arms or legs, she was on her way to the Paralympics, ready to kick ass. I was intrigued reading about how she overcame her disability and became a champion.

"If she can do this, so can I," I declared, after reading Bebe's story.

And just like that, the next day I had another aqua therapy session and completely kicked ass, finishing my forty-five-minute session with hardly a break. I picked up weights from the bottom of the pool with my toes and transferred them to my once-paralyzed arm. I ran faster in the water. I did twists standing on a floating balance board in the water and didn't fall.

I loved every second of this renewed quest to reach my goal of complete recovery. I raised up my workouts several notches, using my arm bike at home and lifting small hand weights in rehab. I did cardio exercise up to my eyeballs. It was all about mental preparation and being a badass. And I was determined to become one. I survived this stroke for a reason, and I had found my inner strength. Pushing my limits became second nature, as I'd tell myself, *This is bullshit!* and do a pirouette on my stroke-affected left leg. After all, I had been a dancer for years. My body was conditioned to do this. I wasn't about to surrender my abilities to a stroke.

In February 2015, nine months after the stroke, I flew to the Grammy Awards in Los Angeles. I was not going to miss the Grammys because I had a stroke. The Grammy Awards are a full day of awards ceremonies and musical performances. I was determined to attend the daytime portion of the awards show, too, as well a few pre-Grammy parties taking place that weekend. It was going to be the Olympics of sensory stimulation, with throngs of people and loud music, but I was ready for the challenge. I wanted to see the friends who provided me with encouragement and stood by me during the worst months and I wanted to support the friends who had been nominated for awards. I hadn't been in an airplane since the stroke and I wondered if I could handle the flight from Boston to Los Angeles. Heck, I thought, with everything I had done up to that point, I could survive a little turbulence over the Rockies.

Mark and I flew to Los Angeles, and I was happy that even though the airline provided handicapped assistance, I felt like an ordinary traveler. I waited for my luggage at the carousel just like I always had before. Mark and I took a cab to our hotel.

The weekend kicked off with several pre-award parties, and I mingled with other Grammy members in my floor-length, form-fitting blue brocade Chinese cheongsam dress with gold glitter combat boots. I toted a ginger ale in my stroke hand, and I didn't mind the blare of the DJ spinning dance music all night long. Mark and I party-hopped to the House of Blues, where yet more friends were playing at a music industry party. I enjoyed myself at two red carpet affairs in one evening in Hollywood.

At the Grammy Awards on Sunday, I walked the red carpet once again, dressed this time in a steampunk outfit I put together: vinyl pants, a corset top, and a veiled retro hat. I brought the wheelchair into the red carpet tent in case it got crowded and I needed it, but I didn't sit in it. I walked the length of the tent dazzled by the glittering chandeliers, excited by all the activity around me. The place teemed with paparazzi, and big-name stars stopped at the media outlets for quick interviews as they entered the pavilion. The reviewing stand was filled with fans cheering for everyone who filed through on their way to the theater.

When the shuttering of media cameras finally subsided, I stood quietly, taking it all in. I had walked the red carpet at a celebrity event in L.A. just months after being completely paralyzed on my left side. I wanted to bow down to Spaulding Rehab right then and there. They had done wonders for me.

Once inside the Staples Center, with Mark pushing my wheelchair, we managed to beat the crowd on the way to our seats. Somehow I survived the night without smashing into anyone with my wheelchair.

After the event, we attended the official Grammys after-party, where I danced for the first time since the stroke. We're not talking bust-out break dances, just only small movements. I wasn't there to push my luck.

I saw my friend Grant there. He had visited me in rehab shortly after the stroke. "This is amazing!" he exclaimed when he saw me on the dance floor. "I can't believe how far you've come!"

What a magical day. Twelve hours of concerts and parties. I could enjoy life again. I was back.

Chapter Twenty-One

H OW COULD I EVER SING again? My voice was crackly and weak.

In July, a few days after I arrived home from rehab, I had received a visit from a good friend, Marcia. Marcia was also a vocalist, and she suggested I take voice lessons from her vocal coach, Vykki Vox. It sounded like a great idea, but I wasn't ready, if I did it at all. I was going to be a difficult student with all of my physical and vocal limitations. My musical skills were gone. It would be like teaching a toddler how to sing, a toddler who fancied herself a professional singer, which made things even worse.

In October, I was ready to enroll in lessons at the Real School of Music in Burlington and learn proper vocal breath support. Vykki Vox would be my vocal coach. Lessons would start right away, for half an hour weekly. Relearning to sing was going to be a massive undertaking. It would take an enormous amount of work and energy to get back to where I was.

Clearly, I was an exceptional case—having had a stroke and a vocal injury—but Vykki was endlessly patient with me. If she could teach someone like me to sing again, she was definitely the Svengali of vocal coaches.

I had to start at the beginning, with the first weeks of my vocal lessons devoted to practicing breathing techniques for thirty minutes with multiple rest breaks in between. For those lessons, I sat in a chair and Vykki guided me through breathing exercises, stopping every few minutes, because the breathing exercises made me lightheaded.

It was as hard as learning to walk again. I could barely get through the vocal warm-up without feeling debilitated or inducing a dizzy spell, and I had zero vocal tone or vibrato. It was like trying to squeeze forty years of developing my skills as a vocalist into a few months of thirty-minute lessons. But thirty minutes at a time was all I could take.

I chose a couple of songs to practice in our lessons. I sang "Hallelujah" by Leonard Cohen, thinking it would be an easy song to start with. Was I wrong! I sounded terrible. But Vykki was optimistic. She believed in me even when I didn't. I chose another song, "Smile," by Charlie Chaplin. I was able to sing the melody with only a few pitch mistakes.

At times, I became quite frustrated at not being able to get through one easy song without my voice cracking multiple times. I was angry. Every song I attempted to sing for Vykki would have been effortless before the stroke. Now a half-hour lesson took most of my energy for the rest of the day.

"I can't do this!" I cried during my first week of lessons, annoyed with myself. "I'll never get my old voice back. I'm done!"

"Ah, but what if you're wrong?" Vykki asked. "What if your voice comes back even better than it was?"

I wanted so badly to believe her.

Maybe she was right. The stroke was devastating, but what if it gave me an opportunity? I'd never had the best vocal habits and I often strained while belting out high notes. I had the chance to relearn to sing correctly and possibly reach new vocal heights. What if relearning vocal technique gave me a better start? What if all I needed to propel my voice to a higher level was better technique? What if I learned to sing even higher notes? For the first time, my "what if" thoughts could actually work in my favor.

A poster hung on the wall in Vykki's lesson room, and during our lessons, I often stared at it. The poster advertised Chick Singer Night 2014, the show I missed because of my stroke. I could see my name listed as a featured singer on the event poster. I had rehearsed, in fact, for that show in this very same school just hours before my stroke. What an easy, carefree life I led at the time, sharing my music with others.

Vykki was eager to help me regain my singing voice, and with her help I made gradual improvements. Each week, I began to lessen the crackling and wavering when I sang. And then my voice would warm up and improve. I could sing the melody even though it was very basic, no-frills. My tone was slowly returning.

An open mic performance at the school was scheduled for November and all of the school's students were invited to participate. "You are making such great progress, Valerie. I think you should do this," Vykki told me when she showed me the information about the event. "I think you're ready to do one song. You can sing 'Smile.' We'll have a chair for you on stage in case you have to sit. Think of it as an introduction to performing again."

I decided to do it. Sort of like the offer to go rock climbing at the Y, there really didn't seem any way I could actually say no.

I practiced singing at home every day. I practiced "Smile" of course, and also a couple of Amy Winehouse songs. Sometimes I used my PA system and microphones during my practice sessions. I was returning to life as a singer.

Singing at that open mic at the Real School of Music gave me a great confidence boost. I had taken only two months of voice lessons and I was already back on stage, even if only for one song. Making a full comeback in every way was clearly within my reach.

The winter days were cold and snow-filled, which halted my daily walks. I relied on the treadmill and elliptical machines at the gym for my cardio workouts. My body *and* my voice were growing stronger, day by day.

With the arrival of spring came hope that I was going to get my driver's license reinstated. I found out that if I ever wanted to drive again, I had to prove to my outpatient therapists that I was capable of doing it; their permission was required for me to take my road test at the Registry of Motor Vehicles. The last time I'd taken a road test I was sixteen years old and my hair took up most of the interior of the Ford Escort testing vehicle. But I would happily take a road test, anything to sit in the driver's seat and have my freedom back.

Months of driving assessment tests in outpatient therapy followed my request for permission to take the road test, and finally I got the go-ahead to apply for reinstatement of my driver's license. The process was lengthy and, like almost everything I faced, involved tremendous patience. I went to multiple hearings at the Registry of Motor Vehicles and waited for hours every time, usually seated in a room filled mostly with people who'd had their licenses taken away. I waited all day on a bench with drug dealers, drunk drivers, and once, an elderly man who had to reapply after losing his license because he suffered from seizures. Each time I went I was asked to return for another hearing and bring more documentation about my condition and my suitability to drive. Criminals walked out of the Registry with their licenses restored the same day they came! That elderly man got his license back in one day, no problem. Not me. I had to practically give the Registry my blood to get my license back.

Finally, just short of one year after my stroke, the day of my road test arrived. I drove very carefully, following the driving instructor's requests, and I left that day with my license reinstated. I was free! Summer was on its way, the days were getting longer, and I would be able to go out when I wanted. I was thrilled not to have to rely on anyone for a ride everywhere.

With summer coming, I also wanted to get toned and muscular. I was lifting small weights in my house every day and wanted to be sure I was going about it correctly, considering all my body had been through this last year. I signed up for a series of personal training sessions at my gym, and Sara, my physical therapist, agreed it was a great idea. My therapy team decided it was time for me to stop outpatient rehab because I was doing so well and continuing my exercise program at home. There would be a few final sessions, and we would say good-bye. I was going to miss rehab and everyone on my therapy team. They had become family to me and I had looked forward to every session. But I was also eager to move on with my life.

Spaulding Rehab arranged for reporters from the *Boston Globe* to do a feature story on me. It wasn't only that I'd had a devastating stroke at so young an age—a small percentage of stroke patients in the Boston area included others around my age—but my stroke and my recovery from it within a year *was* quite a story. I was happy to share my story with the public.

During my final weeks of therapy, a *Boston Globe* reporter interviewed my rehab team—Jerry, Nicole, and Sara—and videotaped me doing physical and occupational therapy. The team commented on my progress and my eagerness to make a complete recovery. It was unusual, and inspiring, they said. They told the reporter how much they had enjoyed working with me for most of the past year. I wished I had a videotape of myself climbing that rock wall and could offer the reporter that to see. To me, that, and relearning how to run using a harness on the treadmill, were two pretty amazing visuals.

Gina Scuderi was a professional bodybuilder and a personal trainer at my gym, and I signed up to train with her twice a week for four months. It would be so different working with someone other than Sara, but I trusted Gina. Gina worked gently and slowly with me, careful to prevent any reinjury of my neck. I told her I couldn't lift more than ten pounds until I passed the one-year mark, which was coming soon.

Gina was awesome, in every sense of the word. She showed me pictures of herself as a chubby teenager and it was amazing and inspirational to look at her now—she was an insanely muscular bodybuilder. If she could transform her body, I could.

Gina pushed me to my limits. With her help, I gained strength and lost any vestiges of the tightness in my left hand and arm. We did things I had never dreamed I could do again. I balanced on one foot doing walking lunges. I did chest presses and bicep curls and other weight-bearing exercises. I carefully studied Gina's movements, just as I had studied the way my visitors moved when I was in the hospital. I was going to do it, and I was going to do it right.

My confidence was improving as a consequence of my work with Gina. When I started training with her, I still had a deep-seated fear of falling, which made my walk a little tentative;

the residual effects of my fall in December weren't gone. The uncertainty in my step was subtle, maybe even unnoticeable, but I felt its nagging presence in the back of my mind. Whenever I went out I would grab hold of whatever I could at every opportunity. But after training with Gina, I felt invincible. My fear of falling was gone at last.

My forty-third birthday was in May. I had thought turning forty was big, but this birthday required an even bigger celebration. I had worked so hard and come so far. My limp had finally disappeared! I was ecstatic. I had an outstanding vocal coach and every reason to try my hardest. I had the stamina to practice singing for longer and longer periods at a time. I could drive myself to appointments, and go anywhere and do just about anything I wanted. I moved my law practice into a new office and Mark was gradually building a good list of clients. Recovery was still my top priority and I was also working on the book I had started writing while in rehab.

Friendship has always been important to me, and being well enough to see friends anywhere but sitting on my living room couch was another new joy that started around the time of my forty-third birthday. I was done sitting and resting and recovering for hours on end.

During those many months of recovery, however, I made some important observations about friendship. A few people I had considered my friends before the stroke completely forgot about me after it. There was not a single text or phone call from some of them. Nothing. I had spent so many years focusing on the good in these people, and during my months of recovery I discovered the truth: They weren't worth a millisecond of my time. I had too much else to do with my energy.

Many amazing friends and family members stood by me through the tough times. They visited me in the hospital the week or so I was there, they came by or called or texted when I was home again. Even acquaintances became wonderful friends. I will always be grateful for them, and all the many other people who let me know they care. When a friend thousands of miles away "massaged" me with her words during my worst days in the hospital and other friends and family showed their big, generous hearts in so many different ways, I found out what real friendship truly is — and just like anything else, I won't accept anything less.

Chapter Twenty-Two

CHICK SINGER NIGHT. THE LAST time I'd sung on a stage was at a rehearsal for Chick Singer Night, before my stroke. Now, Chick Singer Night represented a new beginning. It signaled my comeback.

In June 2015, I was a featured singer again on the Chick Singer Night bill. I was coming full circle after a year fraught with devastation, fear, and hope. *The Boston Globe* was following my journey from rehab and would be at the show for their feature story about me. The performance would be also immortalized in a video available around the world. That video would incorporate their previous interviews with me and my therapy team, videotaped a month earlier. They were documenting my progress. I had to be on top of my game.

Jerry, Nicole, and Sara from Spaulding Rehab were invited to the show. My husband and our parents would be there, along with a couple of fellow stroke survivors who heard about my story, and some supportive fans.

The doubts crept in. *Could I handle this? What if I couldn't sing? What if I got dizzy, or ran out of breath?* The questions swirled in my mind but I refused to allow them to take over and ruin my performance. People were counting on me to entertain them with song. *I* was counting on me, and I wasn't about to let myself down. I had to prove to myself I could do this. I had to show stroke survivors everywhere there *is* life after stroke.

As I sat in the dressing room of Johnny D's Uptown Restaurant and Music Club in Somerville, the venue for the night, I marveled at the series of events that had occurred over the last year. In ways, it seemed like a distant memory — being transferred by nurses from my hospital bed to a wheelchair, spinning with constant dizziness and unable to move my head even an inch to the left or right, walking in a leg brace and then walking with a limp. For days I hadn't been able to swallow, and for much longer than that I couldn't cut my food or properly feed myself. I marveled that I was here, and I marveled, too, that I had wondered whether any of this was possible. It had to be, and it was.

I recounted parts of my story to the *Boston Globe* reporter who came to my dressing room while I waited to go onstage. I wore one of my retro pin-up dresses, a black halter dress complete with black satin evening gloves and a flower in my hair. Mark was in the dressing room with me. He had been with me on this yearlong journey, every step of the way. Tonight was incredibly special to him, too.

Jennifer, a friend and the host of the show, peeked into the dressing room. "Here we go, Val, you ready?" I gave her a thumbs-up.

Jennifer went onstage and introduced me, telling my stroke story to the audience. A hush fell over the crowd, a silence broken by thunderous applause the moment I took the stage, looking beautiful and confident and dispelling all preconceived notions of a stroke survivor. Don't get me wrong — I was nervous. But I was there, and I was ready.

I took the microphone from its stand and said a few words, and then the saxophone solo opened my set. I knew the moment I heard those beautiful, blaring tones open the Otis Redding cover of "Try a Little Tenderness" I was about to sing that I was back.

When the song was done, deafening applause filled the room. Then came the standing ovation, and people cheered. These people were clapping for ME. They were standing up for ME. They had *paid* to see ME.

What a difference a year makes.

But it wasn't just about the passage of time. It was something so much bigger than that. It was my journey from a healthy person to a person stripped of practically every ability. It was about rebuilding myself, shaking off the dust and coming out proud.

When I lay in my hospital bed at Spaulding Rehab almost exactly a year before, I had declared that I would return to the Berklee Umbria Jazz Clinics the next July. I would be able to walk and sing like I had before. It was that near-constant vision of myself back in that setting that helped drive my recovery. On my release from Spaulding Rehab Center, when I sat helplessly on my living room couch, I thought of wonderful friends like Bibi from Brazil and Michi from Italy, and how they were at the Clinics enjoying the Berklee College of Music summer program with all of the concerts and daily performances at the jazz clubs at night. I so desperately wanted to be there that I often had to summon all of my mental strength to focus on the present and take whatever steps necessary to permanently shed my disabilities so I could return to Berklee Umbria Jazz Clinics the following year. I couldn't afford to despair or allow myself to have a broken spirit. I had to do everything in my power to return to Berklee in Italy.

At the time of my stroke and for several months after it, traveling to Umbria Jazz in 2015 was incomprehensible to most people who knew me. I couldn't move my head, there was no way I could sing, and I needed a wheelchair after limping no farther than three feet. My family thought I was insane, but I was fixated. It would be a happy ending to a horrendous ordeal, my ultimate accomplishment, the one that signaled my complete comeback. I was geared up to really sing my heart out for those two weeks, now that I actually had some sort of singing voice again. I started finalizing my travel plans.

Mark couldn't go to Italy with me as he had just come back from a family wedding in China. I would have to travel by myself. Could I do it? Flying had become a production. I couldn't lift my carry-on baggage and I had to inject myself with blood-thinning medication every few hours. How would I navigate the cobblestone streets with my luggage?

My friend Amy offered to go with me, and I happily agreed. We rented a beautiful apartment in the middle of old-town Perugia. I was wild with excitement. Mark would drive me and Amy to New York City to catch our flight from John F. Kennedy International Airport to Pisa, the airport in Italy closest to the Jazz Clinics.

Flying overseas, I was very emotional. I was really doing it! I was on my way to Italy. As we began our descent I could see the city of Pisa below, through the airplane window. Pisa, ironically, was the last place I had visited in Italy before the stroke. My heart fluttered with excited anticipation.

Once the airplane landed, it felt like a dream as I walked down the stairs and onto the tarmac. The heat was brutal; Italy was experiencing a midsummer heat wave, and it felt like we were in a 500-degree oven. But I didn't care. With every step my lamentable ordeal faded further into memory. I might have been walking a little bit slower than before, but otherwise my stroke was undetectable.

Amy and I made our way by taxi to the Hotel Bologna in the center of Pisa. I remembered the feeling of walking the shaded cobblestone alleyways the last time I'd been there, the aroma of freshly baked bread and pastries wafting through the crisp midwinter air, the beauty of rust-colored sunsets over the Arno River and, of course, the view of the infamous leaning tower. I sang a jazz version of "Summertime" around the corner from the Tower, my voice strong and clear.

I typically have a lot of self-confidence, and my way was always to smash through everything I did without looking back. The stroke had shaken my self-confidence to the core, but it was just waiting in the wings to come back.

I knew I couldn't sing like I had. My voice was weakened, still a work in progress. But I was back in Italy, and I felt the adrenaline pulsing through my body, and instead of filling me with doubts, that little voice inside was exclaiming proudly that everything was okay again. The events of the previous year were a blur, a nightmare from which I had finally awakened. The whirlwind of hospital beds, wheelchairs, ambulance rides, and therapies were behind me. I hadn't accepted that all the friends from my old life had moved on without me. I hadn't accepted disability as my "new normal."

Amy and I started by visiting the nearby Tuscan beach town of Livorno. Sitting quietly on the sand that bright summer day, I reflected on my spirituality and where it was taking me next on my life's journey.

After the stroke, I had shunned all things spiritual and religious. Now I wanted those things back. After all, it was my strength of spirit that had ultimately gotten me out of a wheelchair and walking normally again. In the first days after the stroke I had wondered how God could have done this to me, and I realized that God not only spared me from death but gave me the chance to create a new life. A better life. A life filled with the awesome feeling that I was capable of achieving great things. A world of opportunity was open to me. I was strong enough to handle anything. If I could return to Italy, I could go anywhere and experience all that life has to offer. And I wanted it all.

The sun was beating down that day on the beach at Livorno, breathing new life into my soul. I cherished living in the present and resolved not to waste precious energy worrying about how my voice used to sound or how it might sound in the future. What was most important was the present and my genuine self-acceptance. If I focused on the past and the future I'd miss the present. And those moments were precious.

I gazed at the ocean. It was so vast, I wanted to get lost in it. The refreshing smell of salt water perfumed the air. Daylight faded to dusk, and we continued to sit on the beach, taking it all in. The cool sand between my toes felt like satin caressing my feet and welcoming me back into the world. I had missed that feeling, being a part of the world. I am not sure what exactly happened to my spirit on the beach that day, but it was glorious.

Perugia, the capital of the Umbria region, is a medieval hill town perched high in the Umbrian hills. In Old Town, many of its narrow streets and alleyways are steep. You can feel like you're climbing the face of Mount Everest just to get a gelato.

Amy and I arrived in Perugia by train the day after our Livorno beach excursion. In July, the entire city is transformed into an enormous musical Mecca with the Umbria Jazz Festival. Nearly round-the-clock concerts dot the street corners, pavilions showcase emerging and longstanding talented artists from around the world. And the chocolate! Perugia is also known for its intensely flavorful chocolate. The sounds of the music coupled with the aromas of chocolate are dizzying—in a good way.

The apartment Amy and I rented overlooked the main street, Corso Vannucci. Every night I'd lean out the window in the stairwell to listen to a jazz band or a street musician play his saxophone like he was romancing a lover.

My first day at school required an audition song for the class placements. I was brimming with nervous excitement when I entered the audition room to sing before all the vocal teachers. I chose "My Funny Valentine," one of my many signature songs. It was the same song I had performed for my audition the last time I was here. I managed to sing the song almost normally, though it was difficult to hold the long notes or sing as loudly as I did before. But I did it. And it felt amazing.

Twice a day, I walked to school, traveling the steep hills and cobblestone alleyways in extreme heat. It was arduous, and I usually carried a cane to keep from tumbling. As I navigated the narrow alleyways to the Berklee campus, which is on the grounds of an elementary school each summer, I marveled that I was walking in 100-plus-degree heat to take part in a music program after having a paralyzed left side and damaged singing voice. My mind was blown by the thought of it. By the time I reached campus, I was covered in sweat and happy.

True, it was hot, blazing hot. It was so hot my sunglasses even melted. The heat challenged my voice, making it hard to sing. Often, I managed only one or two classes before complete exhaustion set in. I bought a high-powered fan on wheels that I found in a small shop. It even squirted mist. But it was so hot that the fan did little to cool me down. Thankfully, there was a gelato shop on every corner to cater to my Nutella-flavored needs and help me tolerate the heat until I reached our air-conditioned apartment.

At the end of the program, I performed onstage twice at the Umbria Jazz Festival. I was part of a gospel choir and also a contemporary music ensemble with several other students. Both groups performed a few songs each and the crowd loved us.

As I stood on stage, looking into the crowd, I saw a sea of people wanting to hear good music. And I was part of it. I wasn't a stroke patient. I was the old Valerie. Planning to return one day to Perugia and to the music had helped inspire my recovery. The music was a driving force in my rebirth.

On the final day of the program, the director, Giovanni Tomasso, made a special announcement to the students about my condition. He knew my story and was touched by it, especially the impact of the Berklee program on my recovery. He asked me to speak to the students about the healing power of music. After some applause, I took the stage and told everyone what had happened to me and how my passion for music helped to rehabilitate me. Giovanni asked if I had thought of this program after my stroke. "Every day," I replied, holding back my tears.

Now, after two weeks in Perugia, I was returning home to recover every last bit of my voice and embrace the present. Traveling to Italy had again proved invaluable. More than anything else had, it showed me what I was capable of. I learned that I could let go of preconceived notions and accomplish great things. One year before, I never could have withstood walking and studying voice in such heat every day for two entire weeks. Heck, I couldn't even have walked!

I had faced the possibility of a lifetime of disability and had refused it. I may have been beaten down, bruised and battered, but I was steadfast in my resolve, climbing my way out to triumph over a stroke that threatened to steal my body, my soul, and my singing voice.

Today, I understand more about life than I ever have. I know that life is incredibly fragile. Most of us don't truly appreciate what we have until it's gone. And it can be gone, in an instant.

Surviving a stroke put me on a new path. It gave me an opportunity to test my mettle and uncover my inner strength, a strength I didn't know I had. In the end, I discovered that life is what you make of it. I could have chosen to roll over and give up, but instead I chose to rewrite my life and not allow anyone to interfere with my determination to succeed. The journey may be long and it may be difficult, but any road worth traveling in life is worth giving your all. Focus on what you want, with determination and grit. Reach for the stars and dream big. You'll be amazed at what you can achieve.

Acknowledgments

Thank you God for giving me a second chance at life.

I would also like to express my deepest gratitude to the following people:

My parents, Bill and Palma Giglio, for your constant support and encouragement during this entire ordeal. I love you!

My husband, Mark Samson, for sacrificing so much for me. Your constant dedication and devotion during such a difficult time speaks volumes and I am so lucky to have you in my life. If it were not for your unconditional support, I would not have had such a miraculous recovery. You are a very special person and I love you. You are truly one of a kind.

Judith and Paul Samson, for all your help and encouragement. It means so much to me and I am eternally grateful.

My family and friends for all your encouragement and faith in me.

Suzanne Sherman, for all your hard work in helping me put my personal experiences together to craft my story. You are an amazing editor and writing consultant and I couldn't have written this book without your help. I am grateful beyond words.

Drs. Aneesh Singhal and Ming Chai Ding at Massachusetts General Hospital, Neurology Unit.

My therapy team—Sara, Nicole, Jerry, Alex, Ari, and Carla and the entire staff at Spaulding Rehabilitation Hospital. Without your help, I would not be where I am today. I am deeply grateful!

Marcia Macres, for introducing me to the Real School of Music and welcoming me back as a performer at Chick Singer Night Boston.

My vocal coach, Vykki Vox, for working so hard to help me find my voice! You are truly gifted.

My friend Laura Sullivan, for giving me the opportunity to be in your music video for 900 Voices. You encouraged me so much by making me feel like I was still a singer, even when I barely could sing a note. You are a truly beautiful person!

Kristin Gillis Photography, for such a gorgeous cover photo. All your photos are beautiful and you clearly have a magic touch. Thank you for all the phenomenal work you have done for me over the years!

Vintage Girl Studios for the gorgeous author photo. You are very talented and I look forward to working with you again. Your retro-themed photos are outstanding!

Giovanni Tomasso and the Berklee College of Music Umbria Jazz Clinics, thank you for inviting me to return to the summer program. Music heals!

Made in the USA
Middletown, DE
08 August 2016